EPIC TREASURE HUNT ADVENTURES

Published 2024

TABLE OF CONTENTS

PREFACE

EVERYONE loves a good treasure hunt! We've all thought about creating one - something special for a loved one, an inexpensive adventure for a child's birthday party, or perhaps something fun, new and exciting for annual social events. However, treasure hunts have a high mortality rate – most never leave the drawing table. Why? It's a different reason for every person, but most hunts die for lack of ideas or an overall overwhelmed feeling on the part of the planner. The details and complexities CAN add up quickly when creating a treasure hunt, especially if you want to plan something fresh and innovative. However, in this book are supplied enough ideas to fill hundreds of creative, one of a kind treasure hunt adventures for all sizes of groups. That special person's heart will melt when you plan a mini adventure linking Casanova's love notes or perhaps reenacting their favorite fairy tale allowing them to play the prince/princess. Your children's parties will be the talk of their friends when you take them on Indiana Jones style adventure quests and searches for lost treasures. And finally, your friends and associates will marvel at the success of your large treasure hunt events, allowing your guests to roam pirate towns and fight villains from all throughout history. There's no limit to what can be created using this book!

You'll be taken systematically through the entire treasure hunt adventure creation process. Idea after idea will be provided along the way to help spark your own imagination to create fantastic adventures. Discover, explore, investigate and experience the romantic and adventurous possibilities of creating thrilling treasure hunts!

PLEASE NOTE: This book, *Epic Treasure Hunt Adventures*, picks up where our previous book, *Amazing Pirate Treasure Hunts*, leaves off. Although we'll touch lightly on a couple of the more basic topics in creating a treasure hunt in the first chapter of this book, we'll be quickly progressing to the main topic of creating over the top treasure hunt style adventures with a variety of themes that go way beyond what the average person might think of when imagining a 'treasure hunt.'

INTRODUCTION

Why would anyone take the time to write a book about creating treasure hunts? After all, haven't we all been on one (or several) since we were small children, hiding scribbled clues on small pieces of paper throughout the house? It is that simple, right? How could anyone write more than a page and a half (double-spaced) on the subject? Well, we will see…

Twenty years ago, at the age of nine, I began to take a serious interest in treasure hunts. I choose to use the word *serious* here because it was at this time that I began to spend exorbitant amounts of time thinking about different ways to create clues. I was a socially isolating, straight A student who was struggling to find a challenging mental activity that would occupy my time in between assignments in elementary school. I began to think of different ways to mix up words and pictures. I became more fascinated by maps and directions. My teachers were just content that I was sitting quietly.

Once I saw the movie *Raiders of the Lost Ark* that following year, though, I was inspired like never before. The first scene would forever be burnished on my mind and imagination. I dreamed of excavating tombs and temples, of writing in dead languages and losing myself in history. The next several years were spent attempting to recreate the excitement and thrill I felt watching an archaeologist translate a foreign language on a tattered map as he searched for lost treasure.

At the age of 12, my then six-year-old brother was old enough to be a guinea pig for me and my adventures. I enjoyed creating the hunts and he enjoyed going on them. It was a terrific arrangement. Now, I began introducing makeshift booby traps to my hunts. I began experimenting with different ways to treat paper to make it look old and worn. Most importantly, it was at this time that I began introducing *storylines* to my hunts (more about this later…)

In high school I was finally able to break out of my shell and became extremely involved in student government. Now I finally had the opportunity to try out my hunts on groups of people rather than just my brother, that is. In my sophomore year, I first heard about murder mystery dinners and became quickly intrigued with the entire format. I used all the tricks I developed during my years of designing treasure hunts to host original Murder Mystery evenings for several different groups of people. It was during these years I realized the incredible potential of adding live characters to my hunts.

By the time I had graduated from high school, I had set up well dozens of treasure hunts (thanks also to watching the movie GOONIES many times during those four years!) along with several Murder Mystery events.

My course work consumed most of my time during my college years, but I still found some to put on an elaborate adventure hunt or two a year (at least one a year for my brother still). While earning my Bachelor of Arts in Art History, I took several courses of interest (that eventually advanced my hunt designs) such as Japanese and ancient Greek, several archaeology courses, theater production, and studio art. Throughout college, I received phone calls from past participants (or friends of past participants) of my hunts and Murder Mystery dinners; all asking for help with their dinner parties or organization events. These calls gave birth to Quest Experiences, the company my younger brother and I launched in the summer of 1995.

Through Quest Experiences, we renamed our treasure hunts adventures to *quests* in an attempt to express the level of sophistication we were offering. By this time, we were casting actors for roles, working with a costume designer, and purchasing props like fog machines and stage scenery. Most of our clientele were companies looking for something different for their annual BBQ's and Christmas parties, and boy, did they get it!

Simply put, designing these *quests* is my passion.

My hope is that you will see the endless possibilities for creating bigger-than-life adventures for your friends, family, fellow church members, work functions and social organizations. Scattered throughout this book are numerous examples from past hunts. Let them be a catalyst for your own ideas as you are creating.

I have divided this book into several sections. Part I is a comprehensive foundation for creating quests. Here I have attempted to cover every topic that you will need BEFORE you actually begin creating your own.

In Part II are several special tricks and original ideas I've developed over the years to make your quest the most talked about event or activity your guests will have ever participated in. You can also visit our Quest Adventure Society website for more ideas and resources

www.questadventuresociety.com

In Part III, you will actually begin constructing your own quest. Now, I understand the overwhelming temptation to jump to this section first and begin designing right away. This is legal, however, if you skip Parts I & II, you'll be missing all the ideas and tricks that are going to put your event over the top. Part III will assume that you have already read Parts I & II. It will act as a skeleton on which you can put all your great ideas from Parts I and II.

I must note that this book was written from the perspective that you will be planning your treasure hunt adventure for several people (if not a large group.) This is much more difficult than designing a quest for an individual. The ideas and tips throughout this book will work despite the number of participants. If you are considering planning a creative hunt for a friend's birthday or a loved one's anniversary, you should not have a problem adapting any part of this book for a single participant (in fact, there's no trick at all to reduce the number of participants.) I have merely chosen the 'group' perspective for continuity's sake and because planning for groups can be more overwhelming.

To illustrate my points throughout, I will be focusing on three quests that were designed through Quest Experiences, *Nosferatu (a Halloween vampire adventure quest)*, *Dark Fortune* (a pirate themed adventure quest), and *In Search of the Holy Grail* (a Medieval themed adventure quest). Once I began utilizing live characters in my quests, I began to name them as well.

Enough already, let's get started…

PART 1

CHAPTER 1
Where Do We Begin?

"It's always best to start at the beginning."
*Glinda the Good Witch (The
Wizard of Oz)*

"Start at the beginning"
"Yes, and when you get to the end, stop."
*The March Hare and the Mad
Hatter (Alice in Wonderland)*

Who could argue with such wisdom?

As this book is an extension of the our other book, *Amazing Pirate Treasure Hunts*, we'll only touch on the 'basic' treasure hunt format. Perhaps the most popular version of the original treasure hunt idea is where the participant begins with a single clue, usually in the form of a rhyming riddle. This clue will lead them to a new location where another clue is found, repeating these steps until the final location is arrived at. Of course there are dozens of variations on that basic format, but it's arguably the one that everyone is familiar with when they consider what they know about a going on a treasure hunt.

In my experience, it can be difficult to get a group of adults to rally behind these kinds of activities sometimes… not because they are not fun, but more likely because most adults have participated in more of them than they care to mention and rarely do they see something new. Many probably have created one of their own, making it even more challenging to 'surprise' them.

With the basic treasure hunt format, there are several things you can do to enhance the overall activity. These are mentioned below as a way of introducing concepts for future chapters.

USE A STORYLINE – Basically, give your participants an actual reason for engaging in the adventure hunt activity. Rather than saying "Get to the end", tell them they need to find a specific lost treasure, save the city by finding a well hidden bomb or locating a pack of werewolves! They'll have much more enthusiasm right from the get go!

INCLUDE ACTIVITIES – If the only activity you allow for them is the traveling, you're missing out on a lot of fun for everyone! What if once at a location in the treasure hunt the participants had to complete an activity first? What activity? Well, the  possibilities are nearly endless. And if you connect that task to their overall goal (see storyline above) then you'll have the beginnings of your adventure. Much of the adventure you'll create later will involve providing these activities at your locations.

GET CREATIVE WITH LOCATIONS – If your treasure hunt activity is going to be based on arriving at locations, then be very thoughtful about which locations you send them to. Don't make those choices randomly. Additionally, if you can use locations (or create them as we'll see later) that are a part of your storyline above, your adventure will continue to take shape.

ADD SOME HUMAN INTERACTION – We all know that not all of us are social butterflies…but adding even just ONE social interaction with another person along their hunt will provide a level of depth and fun for your participants that you just won't achieve any other way. And, if you happen to allow your participants to interact with a 'character' in your storyline (i.e. someone dressed as a pirate on your pirate themed hunt or someone acting like a spy on your spy themed hunt) then your hunt will start to feel REAL!

Again, these concepts are more thoroughly discussed in our other book, *Amazing Pirate Treasure Hunts*, but it was important to reintroduce them because we'll be expanding upon each of them throughout this book.

CHAPTER 2
You're Going To Give Them Something EPIC!

As we discussed in the last chapter, although there are several different possible formats for the 'basic treasure hunt,' from the simple to the more elaborate, the overall activity remains the same involving the participants going from location to location in a linear fashion, using clues to solve puzzles along the way.

In a *quest,* I attempt to create an adventure through recreating a theme such as spies, pirates, hunting for a werewolf, etc. For example, if I were designing a pirate quest, I would put the teams smack dab in the middle of an actual pirate town with stage props, lighting, sound effects and live characters walking around. The players would need to actually *place* themselves mentally in that environment in order to move along in their adventure. By speaking to different characters, they would learn as a team of some great adventure just waiting to be undertaken. Perhaps they would hear of a woman who had been kidnapped, or of a treasure that waited to be found. No matter the goal, the teams would actually move throughout the physical world I have created (however elaborate due to budget, or sometimes lack thereof).

In a quest I designed for Halloween, entitled *Nosferatu,* my guests traveled through the streets of Crimson Hollow, a fictitious Transylvanian town I imagined. They literally ran from vampires as they searched for the town's few survivors in hopes of learning how to overcome Luther, the Head Vampire. They met a priest in a church, collected some bones from an old graveyard, and even plucked some fur off a sleeping werewolf. It was as exciting as it sounds!

In *In Search of the Holy Grail*, guests worked together to reclaim the infamous chalice for Camelot. They traveled throughout my own English countryside facing wizards, knights, and even King Arthur himself as they raced against time to be the first team to recover the Holy Grail.

One might guess that these were all for children's parties, right? Wrong. In fact, 90% of my quests through Quest Experiences have been EXCLUSIVELY for adults

How will you make your event an overwhelming success? Start with a change of mindset.

Do your best to erase from your mind every preconceived idea you have about what does and does not belong in a quest or treasure hunt. Indulge me for a minute. I promise it will not hurt, much. I want you to remember a time (usually after reading a great book or seeing an exciting movie) when you wished you could have been one of the characters. Have you always wanted to be a knight and rescue a princess from a dragon? Perhaps steal secret foreign plans to avoid a third world war? Ever want to be Indiana Jones or perhaps a Jedi Knight in *Star Wars*?

I will wait while you do this.

Waiting…

Okay, do you have your character? Good. If not, well lie and tell me you do. Chances are that if you felt inspired to be that character, then others have as well and the moviemakers and/or writer did his/her job. Through your quests, you are going to give your guests an opportunity to live out an exciting adventure. How are you going to do that? I'm glad you asked.

We're going to now turn that basic treasure hunt concept on it's head. We're going to take that basic idea of 'following clues' to 'reach an ending' and reinterpret it to create a unique adventure. When one thinks of a great treasure hunt adventure movie, don't we all consider some combination of National Treasure, Indiana Jones and The Goonies? What makes those adventures different from that basic treasure hunt format we just described? Well, a great many things (most of which we touched on in Chapter 1.) We're going to discuss each of those aspects in this book so that you'll be able to create an exciting LIVE adventure for an individual or group.

When I first launched my treasure hunt design company back in 1995 I had a very difficult time explaining to my customers (and my actors/employees) exactly what a *quest* was. This was before the Internet really hit big, before any multi-player role playing game existed online like World of Warcraft and so many others. Essentially, I was creating a whole world with live characters and missions JUST like today's online multiplayer games! The actors played NPC's (Non-Player Characters) that offered the players 'missions' to go on. Once the players helped enough characters, they would have earned enough information to get to the final destination of the adventure. This was all surrounding a main storyline with several smaller storylines (involving each of the individual NPC's.)

Again, it was challenging to explain 30 years ago, but today these concepts are just about everywhere! And that is essentially what I'll show YOU how to create – a LIVE adventure treasure hunt for others to EXPERIENCE.

Much of the concepts described in this book, elements of these live adventures, can be used to enhance your basic treasure hunt – transforming it into something fresh, original and exciting. You can even go crazy by using this book to create adventures that go far beyond the specific theme of a treasure hunt. For example, in a basic pirate treasure hunt, the goal is to find the treasure, right? Well, does it HAVE to be gold and gems? What if someone was kidnapped? Couldn't you utilize all of the basic treasure hunt components to find a person instead of a treasure? I did this once for a large scale Indiana Jones themed adventure where the 100+ participants watched someone get kidnapped by a character villain at a community function. They were each given a 'grail diary' that had clues and puzzles to solve. If they went on the 'treasure hunt' successfully they'd find the kidnapped person and much more!

What if the participants weren't trying to retrieve anything, necessarily? What if their goal was to deliver something important to someone? I used this premise more than once when working with a spy theme. Often times I would tell the participants that they needed to find a spy in the city that was about to walk into a trap. His cover was blow but he didn't know it. They only had a certain amount of time to find the spy and warn him before he walked into danger! I would still use all of the same components included in this book for creating a treasure hunt adventure, I just changed the goal.

What if the players knew of the location of the final destination the entire time but they couldn't 'enter' without completing the adventure first? I've done this before several times, as well. With *Nosferatu* I allowed the participants to know exactly where the vampire's castle was that they had to enter from the very beginning. Oh, except there's a vampire at the door preventing them from entering. The entire adventure involved solving puzzles and completing tasks to prepare to enter the castle…and that vampire guard is there to make sure they didn't enter without having figured out all they needed to first!

Before we go further, there's a basic treasure hunt concept we need to talk about. When we consider a treasure hunt, we typically think of something linear – meaning that it's an unchangeable chain with all of the links fixed in a set order. For the sake of creating a live adventure, we're going to have to bend that rule and perhaps, at times, even break it. We'll still have a beginning…with clues to follow (in some way or fashion)…in order to arrive at a final destination. However, the ORDER for some of those clues to be found may not be important at times. This will create an organic feeling for the players. They'll feel like they are writing their own story and that their path is unique, THEIR very own adventure!

THEMES AND STORYLINES

The theme and storyline will become your main foundational structure. Without your storyline it's like putting up party decorations without any walls or anything else to hang them on. All your clues, characters, **everything** will revolve around keeping your theme and storyline alive.

"Ok, I've worked with themes before…but what do you mean by a storyline?" Once again, I am glad you asked. You are going to be asking your participants to go on an incredible mission. What mission? Well, that is your storyline. Within your theme, you need an overall exciting goal for your guests to attempt (and ultimately succeed in) achieving. Are they looking for pirates' treasure? Are they trying to save a French Aristocrat from the gallows during the French Revolution? Are they trying to smuggle war plans across enemy lines during the American Civil War? Get the idea? All clues and characters will lead and help them on this mission.

In Appendix B, you will find a healthy list of themes along with some possible corresponding storylines. You can pull a theme and storyline directly from this Appendix or use it as a springboard for creating and defining your own. You do not need to decide upon a theme and storyline yet. However, it is IMPERATIVE that you have both BEFORE a single decision is made in designing your quest (Part III). You can change your mind as you read Parts I & II, but you could waste a lot of time by changing halfway through your designing in Part III!

Below are several considerations in choosing a theme and storyline:

First, use something that inspires YOU. That's right, YOU. If you find it exciting, you can make it exciting for others. Simple truism.

Keep your participants in mind. Is it something that THEY could be interested in? (Although, my experience shows that EVERY theme is interesting if presented the right way.)

Keep in mind your surroundings. Will you have access to a wooded area? Perhaps you'll want to search for Bigfoot or discover an ancient idol in India. Do you have access to the top of a tall building? Sounds like a great place to meet a British Secret Service agent.

Although props and costumes (if you choose to use them) are discussed later in this book, it might be a good idea to look around and see what kind of items you have access to. For instance, the fundraiser organizer I mentioned above chose the quest, *In Search of the Holy Grail*. The benefit was being held in a beautiful mansion that had lots of wood and old European style furniture, giving it a possible medieval feel. The theme fit the surroundings and it did not take a lot of decorating!

FORMATS

A quest can be enjoyed in numerous formats.

1 Dinner Party – for groups of 4 to 4000 where guests come to enjoy a meal and an activity – your quest.

2 Car Rally – where teams are in cars. Ideas and suggestions for this format are described later, but the basic goal is to arrive at a final destination after completing the mission over a certain area of a city or larger geographical area.

3 Combination of the car rally and dinner party is when participants do not know where dinner will be held. All guests meet at a predetermined site, the quest begins, and when they have succeeded, (or given up, explained in the car rally suggestions section) they find the location of the final destination where dinner is being served.

4 Progressive dinner. This can make for an exciting evening if organized well. Each course is served at a separate home or location in the normal progressive dinner style. (A progressive dinner is commonly experienced with a group of guests traveling from location to location, eating one course at each stop.) However, the quest unfolds as they figure out which house/location is next. For example, if you chose a pirates' treasure hunt for your theme, you could have your guests meet a mapmaker somewhere in the city who will give/sell them a map and tell them the beginning of a tale of sunken treasure. This map leads to a

location where hors d'oeuvres are served. When the guests leave for their next course, they go to another location on their map where they meet the ghost of a pirate who sank with the ship and learn that he knows where the treasure was secretly hidden before the ship sank. Then off to the next location where salad is served. The guests learn more about the sunken treasure as they travel from location to location, utilizing clues they gather along the way to learn the whereabouts of each course's location.

5   Your format could simply be a party and everyone will participate in the quest at the party's location.

6   A more elaborate quest could be expanded over several days. For instance, when my brother graduated from high school, I planned a week long quest for him to the theme of Batman. During that week he got to live the life of Bruce Wayne as he met different characters for lunch, received phone calls at home and work, and even outwitted villains in order for his high school transcripts for graduation to be properly handled (my storyline).

Let your format enhance your theme and storyline.

BUILDING THE ADVENTURE

Once you have your foundational structure (theme and storyline), it is time to put flesh on them: the tasks and obstacles your guests must overcome to achieve their goal. Simply imagine a movie that would epitomize your theme. What would absolutely HAVE to  be present in the movie to make it true to the theme (or the movie itself, if you chose a specific movie as your theme)?

In *Nosferatu*, my brother and I made a list of things we felt the guests <u>must</u> experience to walk away from the event with the solid feeling that they had just experienced an adventure battling vampires. We came up with the following:

Meeting a Head Vampire (one that controls the others)
Defeating this Head Vampire as the climax
Meeting a character that has been bitten by a vampire
Exploring a graveyard
Consulting a priest
Visiting Transylvania
Being chased by vampires
Discovering a cure for vampire transformation
Translating some Latin text.

You need to create a list like this with your theme. Notice I did not use nouns, but verbs. I never mentioned blood, fangs, or bats. These are not actions, although they are great for building the mood (discussed later). The actions are what will lead your guests on their mission.

To further illustrate, in *Nosferatu* we needed to come up with an overall experience wherein our guests could live out all the above-mentioned actions (as many as we could, that is). We set up the warehouse like a small town in Transylvania (equipped with road signs, the works). Certain parts were sectioned off with black tarp. We explained that each team of four would have to enter this 'small town', complete three thoroughly explained tasks, confront the head vampire in his lair, and then return to the dining area. We told them that vampires had plagued the town for decades and the only survivors left in town are in hiding. The three tasks were to find out the following:

- How to keep from falling under the hypnotic spell of the Head Vampire (Luther).
- How to steal the power away from Luther
- How to escape from his lair once you have done the above.

Sure enough, there were characters in town that knew the above information, but they were difficult to find and did not readily talk without a favor or two being performed for them. For instance, one character had been bitten by a vampire and laid sick in bed. The doctor (an actor I hired) said he needed certain items to make a serum in order to combat the vampire transformation. This same girl had been inside Luther's lair when she was bitten and somehow escaped through a secret exit. She agreed to tell the team where the secret exit was if they would just gather the items on the list (one of the items called for exploring a graveyard - remember from our list of actions?).

As you lay out your actions, you want a balance between those that the teams are specifically told to do (i.e. find Luther's lair, discover a secret exit) with ones that they discover on their own as they work through their mission (i.e. retrieving the items for the sick girl). This creates a feeling of self-accomplishment as they use their problem solving skills to move ahead in the adventure. You see, as I initiated the quest, I told them that they had to enter the town and that they had three goals…how they achieved those goals was up to them. Now, you can probably guess that there was only one way to find out certain information, but it was not perceived this way by the teams. It was up to the team to find the woman. They were the ones that thought of befriending her. They were the ones that found out that Luther himself had bitten her and that she had been in his lair. Their questions led to her asking them the favor. They earned the information. Not clear on some of this? Chapter 3 will help, as it is devoted to the designing of characters.

Do your best to make sure that you have a strong variety in the activities you choose. For instance, with the pirate theme, it might get monotonous if your actions were finding a map, finding a cannonball, and then finding the treasure. Instead, maybe have them gamble with a pirate, steal some deeds from a colonist, and then hire a crew to sail for an island. Get the idea?

CLIMAX

Decide what the most exciting of all the tasks would be. We chose defeating the Head Vampire as the most exciting. With very rare exceptions, the final challenge that the guests take on needs to be the most exciting. They will need to utilize all the skills and knowledge they have collected along their mission. For instance, I had a vampire that would allow participants to enter Luther's lair only once. This means that the team had only ONE chance to defeat him, so they had better make sure that they have done all their 'homework' before they confronted him. This was the climax and tested that they had done what they were supposed to do beforehand. If a team discovered how to keep from being hypnotized and learned how to steal his power but failed to learn where the secret exit was, they would have been trapped inside with a very angry vampire!

In *In Search of the Holy Grail*, the climax came when the teams found Morgana's lair and faced her and her magic. During their journey, they learned what to do and say to combat her spells as she tried to perform them. Once Morgana realized her magic was not affecting them, she threw them in her dungeon, where the teams met the character that was guarding the Grail itself. They befriended him and he let them escape with the Grail and their lives. Definitely a memorable ending!

THE FEAR FACTOR

Fear is an interesting emotion. It can be an unbearable feeling, but it can also be an enjoyable thrill. I've grown to call it the 'fear factor' within a quest. I learned that if I employed some scary task or strong element of fear the participants must endure on their mission, their overall experience would be not only more memorable, but more enjoyable. If you can, make the most fearful task the climax of their mission. When I say fear, I am not necessarily referring to horror (although I am not excluding it, either). Sometimes it simply means putting the participants in a situation that takes them out of their comfort zone. Let me explain.

In *Nosferatu*, it was very easy to come up with the 'Fear Factor' while keeping within the theme. As an added element, I gave each team member a necklace with a crucifix for him or her to wear around his or her neck. The rule was that if any vampire touched them, they had to relinquish one necklace to the vampire. Once the team ran out of necklaces, the team was 'dead' and disqualified. The fear came in when I had a couple of vampires that simply roamed the town pursuing teams. Now, these vampires were instructed to match the speed of whomever they were chasing. For example, if they were chasing some college students, their pace was a lot faster than when they were chasing some of the older participants. The point is that the participants were not aware of these instructions (that I gave the random roaming vampire characters) and always felt like they narrowly escaped the vampires. For a final touch, I had a townsperson who did nothing but run from vampires, yelling for help. Every once in a while, the participants would see him get caught by a vampire. This was enough to keep every player looking over his shoulder the entire time.

Now, what if your theme is the search for pirates' treasure? What if they had to steal something off a big sleeping pirate…if he awoke to see whom it was, he would not trust them with the information he said he would later tell them. Sometimes the task could just mean going into a dark place, meeting a shady figure, or doing something where they could 'get caught.' If you put this in a safe environment, where they do not feel safe, you will insure that your guests have something to remember. If they are searching for the Holy Grail, have them explore a dungeon in the castle. Indiana Jones theme? Have them meet a Nazi soldier threatening to arrest them. Do not be afraid to put the 'fear factor' in your quest. Trust me, it will be the most talked about element of the adventure.

A final note as you decide on the tasks, storyline, climax, and theme… make sure that at the end of their mission, they feel like they've accomplished something more than a treasure hunt. They need to feel like they saved the day. Give them a great mission they could only have accomplished on your quest. In addition, you will want to make sure that EVERYONE finishes. The winning team must be the one that completes their mission first, not instead of the other teams. As an experiment once, I wanted to see what would happen if I created a quest where it was only possible for ONE team to actually complete the quest and win. What I found was that the other teams were disappointed, not that they lost, but that they did not get to help whichever character they were helping at the time and that there were still characters they did not get to meet. However, most importantly, they were disappointed that they did not get to finish their mission. You see, the storyline became more than just a treasure hunt…there were characters' lives on the line and the teams felt it. It would be like watching a great adventure movie, but being deprived of the last 20 minutes…who would not be disappointed?   In announcing the event, say something like "Help save a small Transylvanian town from vampires", "Find Captain Shackelford's cursed treasure", or "Restore the glory of Camelot by retrieving the Holy Grail!" I guarantee that you will have a greater showing if you treat the quest as an adventure rather than just another treasure hunt.

CHAPTER 3
CHARACTERS

When I began experimenting with murder mystery evenings, I really enjoyed creating the characters to set the desired mood. I tried my best to create an open arena without rules, recordings to play, game boards, clue cards, or prepackaged scripts. I merely invited eight to ten guests under the pretense that someone would die before the evening was over. I staged, as realistically as I could, an actual murder (it was all arranged and rehearsed), and then let everyone solve the mystery using whatever skills they brought with them. I really wanted them to feel like it

was real and let them experience solving a real murder. As I struggled to come up with a diabolical murder that would challenge the guests, yet leave everyone saying, "Oh, I can't believe I didn't catch that…" I began to see the power of creating characters. You see, not all of the guests for these evenings were really 'guests.' I always had a small, select handful of guests who were 'on my payroll.' I learned to control these characters to say and do whatever I needed them to in order to create the perfect murder. I was able to write a murder mystery as controlled as a novelist while the guests marveled at how 'everything just seemed to come together.' When I transferred this idea to my treasure hunts, a brand new dimension was added to my adventures.

WHY INSERT CHARACTERS?

Do not let this addition intimidate you. This is what everyone will be talking about long after your dinner party, fundraiser, or youth event. Characters may not seem worth the effort at first, however, if you were creating an exciting adventure with a storyline, characters are essential and the return for your effort is astronomical. The following are a few characters that I have used in *Dark Fortune* and their part in the adventure:

<u>Bartholomew</u> was a drunken pirate in a tavern. He had overheard an argument in the Captain's Quarters on board the S.S. Dark Fortune just before it mysteriously sank. Although a bit on the incoherent side, he does not mind telling the teams whatever he knows as long as they keep his whiskey glass full.

The barmaid was named <u>Clarise</u>. She did not tolerate any drunkenness in her tavern and threatened all offenders with a free night in the local jail. She seemingly did not know anything about anything, except how to keep people's glasses full.

From <u>Willoughby</u>, the mapmaker that sold the teams the map, they learned of a crazy woman who mumbled about an argument she was in with the Captain aboard the SS Dark Fortune. She, they also found out, was being held in a prison cell for the time being.

The crazy woman (who turned out to be mute from the shock of the sinking experience) was named <u>Rose</u>. Rose knew the actual longitude on their map of where the lost treasure was located. However, how would they get to speak to her, she was in prison?

The prison was not coincidentally right next to the tavern. Teams figured out that if they made enough commotion in the bar, Clarise would make good on her word and summon a soldier to take them to a cell in the prison area, where, it just so happened, they would end up sharing a cell with good ol' Rose.

This entire chain of events took about 15 minutes for the teams to experience, from when they first buy the map, to meeting Bartholomew, to learning where Rose was, to getting thrown in jail, to finding out the information that they needed, to even escaping from prison soon after. Now, not a single character told any team that if they acted drunk in the tavern they would get to find out the longitude, the teams figured it out for themselves, and that made all the difference in their adventure. If done properly, each team will finish feeling as though their own experience was unique to everyone else's and that if they did it over, they could have done it entirely differently. You know better, but they do not.

CHOOSING YOUR CHARACTERS

You'll choose your characters when you are designing your quest. They come out of necessity. You might find that at some point you'll need to give your teams a map. Well, how will you give them that map? It looks like you might need a mapmaker in town to sell them one…and slowly your world/ community builds.

Ideally, you would have an unlimited supply of professional actors (like the movie *The Game* with Michael Douglas) but that is likely not the case. I have worked with casts of 1 to 30. The number of characters you have does not determine the level of your success, what you do with them does. I've found a good ratio of characters to players is one character for every two <u>teams</u>. Now, I have not said one character for every two <u>participants</u>, which brings us to the subject of teams.

TEAMS

I have planned quests for both crowds and individuals over the years. I have experimented with many ways of grouping participants together. This is what I have found to be CONSISTENTLY true for all age groups:

A single participant – If he were the only one participating in the quest, I would still advise having someone going along with him, even if that means you. Funny things happen. Exciting things happen. It can be disappointing for someone to laugh and/or get scared all alone.

Teams of two – This can potentially work very well for smaller groups. I have found, though, when a disagreement occurs about what to do or where to go and there is no one to 'break the tie' the pair may return a bit on edge.

Teams of three – Not ideal at all. It definitely breaks the ties, but it also creates the 'third wheel' effect in a most powerful way. Two people end up getting more excited than the third, leaving the third out of several, if not all decisions. When all is said and done, your participation ratio will drop from 100% to 66%.

Teams of four – The best for groups of 15 or more. The dynamic of four seems to solve all problems. Although there is an even number of votes when deciding on certain actions, the individuals tend to be more open minded to possibilities when there are more people involved. No one is left out, for if two members are speaking to each other, two others are able to engage in a conversation of their own.

Teams of five and larger – Forget it. Enter the 'committee' effect. Teams hardly achieve anything as a group because they cannot agree on any action. Factions within the group form and things can get ugly.

You could very well create a quest that is so fantastically different, that some of the above guidelines might not apply.

…

Now, where were we…oh yes, character to team ratio. Again, an ideal number to try for is one character for every two teams. Why? Mostly for the sake of traffic. By traffic, I am referring to the actual movement of your guests on your quest. This is deceptively more important than it might seem at first glance, so much so that I have dedicated a separate section to this very topic later on in the next chapter. You see, if you have a character that demands five minutes of every teams' playing time, and you have 10 teams playing, that leaves 50 minutes straight of this character talking to teams, one team at a time. Why one team at a time? It is explained more thoroughly in the next chapter, but for now just imagine the chaos of four teams trying to ask a single character multiple questions, all at the same time! (See the Rules section in the Chapter 5.) Now, if this character is one of the first you would like your guests to meet, that would mean that at about the time one team is finishing up their quest, another team is still in line waiting to speak to their first character. If you are not able meet this kind of ratio, have no fear. In the traffic control section in the next chapter and in Part II, (Chapter 12 - Characters Without Actual Actors) you will find other means to occupy your adventurers without the need for as many characters.

FINDING PEOPLE TO PLAY CHARACTERS

Depending on your resources, this can be a very challenging task. Let me dispel a couple of fears first. The best people to play your characters are not necessarily trained actors. It depends entirely on the personality of the character that you want to bring to life. There have been numerous times when I needed to create a character entirely around what I thought a certain person could pull off, because of a severe lack of volunteers. In no way, however, am I insinuating that the quality of the character suffered from it. Most of the actors I've hired were not actors at all, but rather personality types who enjoyed having fun for a little bit of cash. If I needed a boisterous barmaid, I simply found that "character" (or someone that COULD be that character) in my life and asked them to participate. You would be surprised how many people <u>would love</u> to participate when you put it in the right light. With few exceptions, I have not had problems finding enough people to play my characters (some even had a hard time accepting money for their time because of the great fun they had! A few individuals actually refused once the event was over.)

Another thing to clarify is the degree of difficulty involved. In your own mind, you have to arrange the relationships of your entire little world…who knows what and to what degree. Where certain things are hidden. How long. When. Why. How. AHHHH!!! However, your characters do not. This is worth repeating. Your volunteers/ actors do not have to know anything beyond what their own character would know, which is usually very little. I found out early on that the actors get confused about what information they were and were not allowed to release to the teams. They actually knew too much. The best thing is to tell each actor what he needs to know for his specific task only. This way, there is only a fact or two to remember. For example, the only instructions that I gave to Clarise, the barmaid in the previous example, was that teams would be coming into her tavern and that she needed to treat them like customers. In addition, at some point in serving them, warn them about getting drunk in her tavern and about the possibility of spending the night in jail over it. I also told her that if teams DID cause a ruckus, then she needed to follow through with her threat, and call a soldier of the neighboring prison to take them away.   She literally knew NOTHING MORE, which is exactly what Clarise would probably have known if she had actually existed. The actress playing Clarise had a great time enjoying her role, watching teams trying to act drunk and getting a little rowdy attempting to get themselves thrown in jail. It was not until after the quest was all over, when all the actors got together, that they got a chance to compare notes to figure out what exactly happened. Everyone had fun telling their fellow cast members what their crucial piece to the adventure was.

So, who would qualify as a potential actor/actress? Family members (young and old), friends, co-workers, casual acquaintances, anyone and everyone. It depends entirely on your characters. Preferably someone reliable and who is quick on their feet. It is okay to have a volunteer who is a real stick in the mud…providing you give them a character that would fit that personality! See what I am getting at? Create the world with what you have.

TRAINING YOUR ACTORS/VOLUNTEERS

Communication is the key. Once you have approached your potential volunteer character, set a time over coffee when the two of you can be alone without distractions. Prepare for this meeting ahead of time so you will know everything you need to say, and ONLY what you need to say. Remember, the less they know, the easier it is for them and chances are the more successful they will be. If they want to know more, tell them enough to satisfy their curiosity without giving away too much. Inform them that when the event is over you would be more than happy to explain the entire story.

Write it all down for them. Make it clear on a single sheet of paper everything that you are discussing with them. They can reassure themselves that no matter how nervous they might get, that they know exactly what is expected of them and they only need to know their small part.

Make sure they understand that they need to be ON TIME, no matter what time you set. Being late, even if only minutes, will not be an option. Have them arrive IN COSTUME, if possible, ready to go. If they need help with costumes, then make sure that they have what they need according to your expectations for the character.

Okay, so you have chosen your volunteers/actors and they understand exactly what they are supposed to do and what relevant information they possess that the teams will need. However, how quickly should they reveal this information? Would it be best to have a character simply walk up to a team and blatantly tell them a key piece of the story? Since more than likely there will be more than one team competing, I developed The Reward System. This is described as having all your characters in an initial state of a severe lack of awareness and interest in the teams that are invading their town/world. Therefore, it is up to the teams to initiate the conversations, to figure out how to 'get to know the character.' The stronger the effort that the actor feels the team is making to really try to get into the story, the more quickly the actor will reveal what he knows. For instance, if a team walked up to the drunken pirate Bartholomew in the above example and just started saying things like "Can you tell me how we can win this treasure hunt?" then he might respond by passing out on them. However, if the same team came in, sat down at his table, and told Clarise to pour a glass for everyone at the table (including old Bart), I think they would have Bart's attention. The more the teams play along, the more they should be rewarded with time and information. You see, they are on a race against others. The way to penalize a team is to waste their time. The way to reward them is to give them exactly what they need quickly. In the Rules section, this is discussed further, but you would be surprised at how quickly the teams understand and get into this type of playing. Remember the former example from *Nosferatu* about the sick girl who needed certain items to combat her vampire transformation? Remember I mentioned there was a doctor that was guarding her bed making sure that she got her rest and that she didn't have any visitors? One team, when stopped by this doctor, had a member that thought quickly and immediately rustled up some fake tears and explained to the doctor that Durrell (the sick girl) was her sister and they had some important news from their dying father. The actor that played the doctor thought that that kind of creative thinking was worth rewarding and let them through without any more delaying. This team got the most out of the adventure and, not coincidentally, was the first team to finish.

SOME FINAL NOTES

Do your best to have a variety of characters' personality types. Even if all your characters are pirates, they can be different personalities. A big gruff type, a small weasel/pick-pocket, a compulsive liar, a drunk, a scam artist, a stutterer, etc. Perhaps you could have a tavern keeper, the head of a brothel, a couple colonists, some Spanish soldiers, a sea captain, a couple children....let your variety create your realism. In real life, there are all types of people. Your quest should reflect that reality.

Name all your characters. Even if their names are never mentioned, it will help the actor be more convincing if he/she feels like their character actually exists. It will also help you as you are planning and creating.

A character does not have to have anything to do with what the participants need to finish their mission. In *Dark Fortune*, I had two college students who did nothing but roam the streets of the small town dueling each other. They knew nothing about the storyline or what the teams were trying to accomplish. They merely continued fighting every time they saw they had an audience. Sometimes they chose a frequented pathway to block for a couple of minutes just to add an obstacle for the teams. It did wonders for adding atmosphere. Another character was held in leg shackles near a much-frequented part of town. Above his head was a sign that read "Liar." I explained to this character that his sole job was to stop teams and try to delay them, typically by trying to elicit help from his bonds. Despite the sign, you would be surprised at how much time the teams wasted with this person. Halfway through the quest, most of the teams had caught on to the fact that he actually knew nothing and was only a distraction. He was probably the most memorable and talked about character of the entire quest.

CHAPTER 4

Those Not So Fun Logistics

1.

HOW LONG SHOULD IT LAST?

Timing a quest can be a difficult skill to master. Unfortunately, it takes a lot of practice to get the timing down – to know how long it will take the average person to complete a certain task. However, I will share with you everything that I learned on the subject.

My most successful group quests have had the first place team coming in about 55 minutes after starting, and the last place team taking one hour and 15 minutes. Sounds specific? You are right. I have been hired on several occasions to fit my quest in between dinner and an awards ceremony. I was given only minutes for a buffer. I learned under a lot of stress how to plan my quest down to the minute. Since you will be doing the planning yourself, you can leave yourself as much time as you need. However, I still hold to my 55/75 minute rule. Anything under about 55 minutes, the teams feel like it's over too quickly…however, as soon as you reach 1 ¼ hour, teams start getting tired, losing their excitement. If you can come somewhere close to these periods, you will have a very satisfied crowd that will be begging for more!

If you have a car rally, you may need a little more time due to the amount of driving involved. However, do not use this as an excuse to make it over two hours. Your participants will not forgive you.

If the quest is for an individual, then use what you know of the individual to decide on the length of time. When it comes to groups, you have to rely on averages. When it comes to individuals, you have more freedom to adapt.

A great way to time your quest is to break all your tasks down and write down how long it will take in minutes to complete each small task. It is not as hard as it sounds and, I will step you all the way through it in Part III.

What do you do if it is taking longer than expected for the teams to complete their mission? I have been known to pull a couple of actors aside in between their interactions with the teams and explain they need to release their information quicker (especially if lines are forming!) Sometimes, due to unforeseen circumstances, I have instructed actors to blatantly tell teams certain information immediately just to move things along.

What if the reverse is true? What if teams are taking no time at all figuring out your quest and you anticipate that the first place team will be coming in within 30 minutes? Tell the reverse to the actors. Once I explained to the mapmaker during *Dark Fortune* that he needed to somehow slow people down at his stop. My quick thinking actor suddenly developed a stutter. It took a bit longer for each team to get the information they needed. Feel free to make these types of decisions. Remember, it is your world. You created it. At the end of this book I have detailed exactly what to do the evening of your quest, so have no worries there. You will be more than equipped to handle just about everything that could possibly come your way.

Some final words on timing. Be aware of the starting time. Have a timeline so you and your actors know exactly when everything will start and finish. People will always be late. Being on time should be the most emphasized detail when communicating to your guests. Explain to them that it is imperative that nobody be 'fashionably late.' Another trick is to plan a small hors d'oeuvre or activity BEFORE the quest begins. Then, if someone is late, they may miss something, but it will not be the quest.

Why is it so important that nobody is late? Imagine you pull 50 participants together and explain the rules to everyone on how to conduct themselves in the small pirate town you created. You spend a little time making sure that everyone is in a group. You have a small little dramatic presentation to kick off your adventure for everyone to see and get a better understanding of what they are dealing with. You have answered questions and everyone is ready. The teams enter the town and your adventure begins! You are now roaming around your creation, watching everyone enjoy themselves, and fixing whatever small problems occur. So far, a very successful evening. Then, suddenly, five late guests arrive and really want to join in. You notice their deadly member number is five and wished they had arrived earlier, for you were previously forced a to release a team of three. They are full of questions, all of which were asked by others when you explained the rules the first time. Additionally, they are at a severe disadvantage in understanding exactly what it is that they are about to participate in without you taking time away from your quest (hoping that everything is running smoothly) as you take an additional five minutes to explain what they need to do. Now your oversized, rag-tag late team is 20-25 minutes behind everyone else and probably won't get a chance to finish (which is, remember, bad), and you have taken precious time away from making sure that your quest is running smoothly for those who arrived on time. Do what you need to do to make sure that when you begin introducing the activity, everyone who is going to participate is present, attentive, and ready.

WHERE IN THE WORLD AM I GOING TO HAVE THIS THING?

That is a great question that needs to be answered early. Is it going to be spread over a city? Contained in your home? Will you have access to a church facility? Maybe just part of it? You need to answer these questions when you are deciding how many guests you are going to have. You need to have specific boundaries that you can communicate to your guests. For instance, if you chose a car rally style quest, make sure that you keep the boundaries to a specific town, city, or something else similar of your choice. If the participants do not understand what the boundaries are, there will most definitely be a few teams who will end up in Timbuktu. Take my word for it. In regards to homes and facilities, simply explain beforehand which areas are available and which are not. You can do this by marking off certain areas with a colored ribbon, detailing them as inaccessible on their maps, or simply explaining to them during the question and answer period.

Once you have your area, make a map of it for yourself. Make several maps. If spread over a city, drive around and get to know all the nooks and crannies of what is available. Same goes for if in a home or facility. Explore broom closets, doors, back entrances, hallways, stairs, rooftops, gardens, porches, EVERYWHERE.

When exploring your space, note with a big asterisk any (what I call) *circulars*. If you are planning a car rally, this doesn't apply. If your guests are on foot, read this section several times. A circular is any area, room, or closet that has two means of entry/exit. For example, a kitchen might have an entrance from the living room as well as one from the garage. These are very important for controlling traffic. They also add some very interesting ways of building a story. For instance, I had a dungeon scene in *In Search of the Holy Grail.* The teams entered through one door and were able to escape from another (once they learned how). The appearance was that teams would enter the dungeon, but never come out. It worked terrifically. It is okay if at this point you have no idea what you will do with them. That will come later. The main thing is to identify all circulars that are available to you.

GROUP SIZES

The size of your group will greatly change how you design your quest. What you can do for small groups would be an organizational nightmare with large groups and what you create with large groups could be down right impossible for small ones.

With large groups, it is easier to round up more characters. So, you can add a greater sense of detail as you create your world. With larger groups you have to be more mindful about traffic and making sure that there are not any 'bottle-necks' anywhere. Also, space is usually an issue and needs to be addressed (see Traffic Control section below).

With smaller groups, 15 or so, you can have more of an intimacy between your characters and your participants. However, it can be difficult to find a place that will hold an entire adventure for just 15 people

Perhaps, the biggest issue to deal with when involving larger groups is…yep, that's right, traffic control.

TRAFFIC CONTROL

Why did I mention it so much before actually getting to this section? I wanted to express how integral this factor is to all that you create. I have had some wonderful ideas that blew up in my face because I neglected this issue.

Let me explain further. You are creating an adventure for a team, an overall experience. The way to kill that feeling is to jam one team next to another who is doing the same thing. Don't understand? Each team is going to want to feel like their individual adventure is unique…when they overhear others talking about the exact same experience, it kills it. In addition, you want teams to be able to talk to each character alone. The other teams need to be away from earshot or cheating can occur.

A lack of traffic control can also breed frustration. Waiting in line is never fun. Back tracking is never fun. Having too many people in a small area is never fun.

So, how do you have good traffic control? There are several ways.

First, avoid small, tight dead ends. Otherwise, when a team goes in, they must come out the same tight way (usually forcing other successive teams to one side while they squeeze through). Second, make use of wide-open areas for the opposite reasons above. Thirdly, utilize your circulars. Circulars can keep a constant flow of traffic coming very easily, which is what you want. Teams come in one way, and then exit another. An ideal set up. An example of this was when the teams met Morgana in *In Search of the Holy Grail*'s climax. Once they defeated her spells, they were moved to a different room (the dungeon) then out another door (escaping from the dungeon) back out to the original playing area.

Have characters that are traffic control characters. The doctor that I had stationed near Durrell, as mentioned earlier, was nothing more than traffic control. He was there to detain teams from talking to Durrell until the previous team was done speaking to her. He had no idea why they needed to speak to her (unless they told him) nor what Durrell would tell the team in return. He only knew that his job was to make sure that only one team spoke to Durrell at a time.

The average age of your participant is important when dealing with traffic control. Typically, an older crowd will want to move at a more leisurely pace than a younger one. My rule of thumb has always been this: the younger the crowd, the more physical the activity. Later  on, when you actually design your quest you will walk your adventure. Then you will get a greater feel of how tired your guests may be.

If you are having a bit of trouble hitting that character to team ratio, you may have to be a little more creative as you design, leaving activities for your teams that do not involve as much character interaction (see Chapter 12). To keep traffic to a minimum, you might have a character send teams on long errands, perhaps to collect a long list of objects or information pieces. In this way, the teams are kept busy without demanding a lot of time from your few characters. An example of this can be seen in *Nosferatu*. In order for teams to get Durrell to help them, they first collect a number of items on her list for her doctor to make an anti-serum to fight the vampire transformation in her body. This led the teams all over town looking for things like wolf bane, cemetery bones, and the hair from a werewolf.

A freebie tip…I did attempt once, and I want to emphasize ONCE, the idea of introducing a maze to the playing field. In one of the pirate quests, I put up a series of ropes throughout the warehouse creating a small maze in town. I thought this would add some fun, as the team maneuvered through town, remembering how to get to each station. However, it backfired. Teams were very anxious to get to where they wanted to go and having to dealing with the maze led to frustration. If you do use one, be aware that a lot of mental energy will be spent simply maneuvering about and that your mental challenges and puzzles should be eased accordingly.

CHAPTER 5

Problem Solving

Over the years and the many, many quests I have created, one thing is certain…I have had my share of problems. One thing that you can plan on is the unexpected. Things will happen that you did not plan for, but that does not mean that you cannot prepare for them.

RULES

I have found when the teams understand the rules before they begin, 95% of your problems are solved. I learned early on to commit the rules to paper and to make sure that every team begins with a copy. Keep the number of rules to a minimum. When the teams are heavily involved in your story, they are not going to remember a lot. In addition to committing them to paper, I also thoroughly explain them to everyone just before the actual quest begins. Everyone can ask whatever questions they might have. Below I have listed rules that I have initiated before for various quests. Some may apply, some may not. At least you will be able to get some ideas of what kinds of rules you might need for your quest.

- Teams must stay together. If teams do not stay together, your traffic increases. Think of the 'carpool' principle.
- There is no tampering with clues. (Punishable by death)
- No running. Obviously this one can be difficult to govern. However, in small spaces, running can actually cause an accident.

- Only one team may speak to a character at a time. It breeds a lot of bad feelings if Team A did all the work to get a certain character to confess some needed information, only to have Team B overhear and gain the same information without the work.
- Stay within the boundaries. Here is where you would lay out the actual playing area so that you do not have any teams that venture far away from the action.
- Under no circumstance are you to touch a character. This eliminates several possible problems that could make things quite ugly (see the Alcohol section) Explain to the teams that the quest is a mission of wits, not of muscle.
- Treat the characters like who they are. If encountering a King, then bow in his presence and give him the honor that he deserves. Explain that the more the teams treat the characters how they should be treated, the quicker the character will give them the information that they need.

- A special note for car rallies…Bring a stack of envelopes to the quest. Give each team an envelope for everyone on the team to put their driver's licenses in, and then have each team seal their envelope. The teams are to hold onto this envelope during the entire quest and will be disqualified if they finish the quest with an 'opened envelope.' You see, if, by chance, the team tries anything tricky on the road such as speeding or cutting other team members off, they are candidates for being pulled over by a police officer. At that time, they would have to break the seal on the envelope to show the officer the driver's license of the driver.

CHEATING

I could never list all the ways that a team can cheat, but I will mention the common ways I've seen over the years.

- The tampering of clues. Make sure that every vital piece of information is secured. There were quests years ago where I had a note taped to a railing or a rock as a clue. What I found was that there will always be one team who thinks themselves clever when they rip the clue apart or throw the rock over the cliff or down the road. The solution is simple…NEVER have a clue that can be tampered with.

- Teams splitting. This is actually an innocent form of cleverness that can be initiated by the team. It involves the team splitting into separate groups to split the tasks and then meet at a rendezvous point. There are three possible solutions. One is to have your quest in a linear format (when all the actions on the quest lead directly to a specific other action – a predetermined order you have set up ahead of time) where each team is presented with only one task at a time. The second is to inform each character to not speak to a team unless the predetermined number of teammates is present. The third is to tie the team's members together (however, this will not work for car rallies…unless you give the teams a lot of slack between each team member.)
- Harassing of characters or stealing clues. If a team must negotiate with a character to get a certain object like a microchip or microfilm and they are finding themselves unsuccessful, the option could be open to actually manhandling the character to get what they want. I will admit, this has only happened a couple of times, but it was very ugly when it did. Fortunately, I had a back-up plan. I had another character armed with a toy gun nearby. When the manhandled character explained the situation to the armed character, the team was soon followed, 'shot', and disqualified. We were able to 'take care of cheaters' and still stay within the theme.

Although it is good to mention the different ways cheating can occur, it is also possible to attack cheating or irreverent behavior at its core… the motivation to cheat in the first place. The following are a few suggestions that greatly reduce the presence of cheating.

- Clearly explain the rules and give each team a copy before they begin.
- Have consequences for foolish behavior. For instance, in one of the pirate quests I designed, I armed each team with three Letters of Marque. A Letter of Marque in history was an official document from a nation's King allowing the owner 'legal' piratical activity on that nation's wartime

enemies. This document was greatly desired by all characters in town. Since the teams were not armed with any weapons, their only defense was to negotiate for their lives with these Letters. For instance, if a team got a little too rowdy with a pirate and were soon threatened with being shot, they might offer to give a Letter of Marque to the pirate in exchange for their lives. This allowed each team three 'lives' to make costly mistakes. After that, if they were 'killed,' then they were disqualified. Now, of course, if a team committed an act that was flat out worthy of disqualification, I would merely have a pirate walk up to them and shoot them without the opportunity to negotiate for any documents.

- Have a good story. When the teams feel like they are actually part of a story, they forget they are racing against others, thus eliminating much of the competitiveness.

ALCOHOL

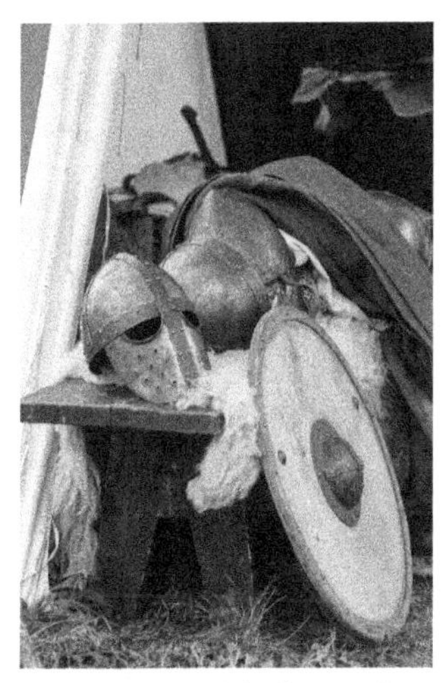

I do not intend to get into a moral debate over the consumption of alcohol, however I will firmly state that it is a dangerous addition to your quest. The first time I held a quest where the participants were drinking just before the quest began ended in tragedy. Alcohol can make the most responsible person do irresponsible things. The actors I hired were put in harm's way on several occasions and I eventually had to cut the evening short. I swore I would never have a repeat of such an experience. However, one year later, I did have a repeat incident and it brought me to a deeper conviction for the absence of alcohol for all future quests.

Consuming alcohol can impair a person's problem solving abilities. By consuming alcohol, I do not mean getting drunk. Even a small amount of alcohol consumption can impair one's ability to think through a situation. Because a team must rely on their problem solving skills to correctly (and safely) navigate their mission, it is easy to see where problems can arise.

Additionally, some people can become much more aggressive when they have been drinking. Aggression mixed with impaired problem solving skills can be disastrous to your quest.

So, what do you do if you would like to have alcohol at your function? Simple. Serve the alcohol only after the quest is over.

So, what do you do if you must serve alcohol before the quest begins? Simple. Do not plan a quest. Have a different activity. Trust me, the odds are stacked severely against you for having a successful event.

CHAPTER 6

The Day of the Event

So, you have planned and created, anticipated everything that could possibly go wrong and the event is finally here. All your hard work is about to pay off as you watch your guests have the time of their lives.

I have comprised all the details and problems that can occur on the day of the event. Again, I've had almost everything go wrong that could go wrong over the years between all of the quests that I've designed. Take my suggestions seriously as we go through them together. They could save not only your sanity, but also the entire event.

This may sound cliché, but above all get a good night's sleep the night before. There is a procrastinator in all of us, two in me, actually. Because of my capacity to procrastinate, I have had several long nights just before many of my quests. I have been up all night on several occasions, trying to get everything done before the quest began. Each time I procrastinated, I put the success of the quest in jeopardy. If I am not at my most alert, it is easy to forget the quest's many details. In later years of quest creation, I have made a promise to myself to NOT work on any part of the quest the day of the event. That means preparing ahead of time. Then, you are able to go for a walk in the park, visit the beach, or just stay at home reading a good book before the event. This is greatly needed mental preparation to solve the problems that could arise when your event actually begins.

A further word about preparation. A successfully created quest will run itself. In Part III of this book you will spend a lot of time creating an entire adventure for your guests to participate in. You will create characters that will guide your participants through the story. Then, you will train your actors to guide your guests according to the character they are portraying. When the quest begins, you will find that you will not have a lot to do. You have created a living, breathing organism and your job is to sit back, watch, and enjoy seeing your story and characters come alive. In this light, do your best to make sure that you do not have any responsibilities during your quest. Divorce yourself from the food issues, parking problems or any other mental distractions you may be tempted with.

A final note…make sure you are wearing comfortable shoes. You will be doing a lot of walking during the event.

YOUR GUESTS ARRIVE

By the time your guests arrive, you do not want to show the slightest bit of anxiousness to anyone. Your guests are about to participate in an event (whether you've informed them ahead of time or not) that will be different from any other activity they have participated in before. When people engage in unfamiliar activities or situations, there is a certain degree of uncertainty and anxiousness. They will be looking to you, their host, for guidance in how to emotionally handle the situation. Smile. Be confident and joyful (unless the theme or mood dictates otherwise).

HOUSTON, WE HAVE A PROBLEM

Sometimes a problem can occur before your quest begins.

Oh my gosh…I forgot the (blank). That blank could be a piece of paper with your timeline; the crucial missing pieces to the maps the teams need, or even your rules sheets. What do you do? Well, hopefully you live close enough to the event site (assuming the event is not in your home) that you can make a quick call and have someone deliver it to you. The real solution, though, is having a complete checklist of everything you need to have in your car before you leave the house. Pack your car the day before. Make your list and check it twice. Forgetting the wrong item can be disastrous. The first time I held the *In Search of the Holy Grail* quest, I forgot a major piece, Merlin's book of spells. It was a book of several sheets of paper (all the same) I had bound that had the spells the teams would need to combat Morgana's powers for the climax….VERY important. I was about two hours from home and unable to get them. Luckily, however, I did have my original in the car and was able to run to a super market to make last minute copies. They did not exactly look like pages from an old book, but hey, beggars cannot be choosers. I learned from that experience to make a list and pack the car the night before so that NOTHING is left behind.

Oh my gosh…everyone is late. No problem, hopefully. See later in this chapter where I have given some suggestions on how to quicken or slow a quest down.

Oh my gosh…one of my actors has not shown up. This can be a problem. First of all, do not panic, yet. Unforeseen things can happen, usually at the most inopportune times. We cannot help car failures or other such emergencies. However, you have 50 guests who are minutes away from a quest that is not going to happen unless you find a replacement for the crucial character that suddenly broke his leg fixing his car that afternoon. What do you do? First, ask yourself if you can live without the character. Is there something you can tell to a couple of the other characters so that the teams can at least finish? If you can get away with it, try this approach. If the character is just too crucial, attempt to pull an actor from another character that is not as crucial. Quickly give them a crash course on what they need to do to make sure the teams will be able to finish. If every character you have is crucial and irreplaceable…the only other suggestion is to explain to the guests that due to a minor problem, *you will* be replacing one of the actors. Why tell your guests? Tell them so that they will understand that you will be a 'different' person in the quest, not yourself. If you know in advance, you can work this character into your evening as you talk to your guests before the actual quest begins.

GETTING THINGS STARTED

Okay. You are ready. Your guests are ready. Your characters are in place. It is time to pull everyone together. Before you begin a

Preshow for your quest, it is best to explain the rules and exactly what your guests are about to participate in. You see, the 'movie' has not started. Now's the time to talk to your guests <u>before</u> they get engrossed into your storyline. Explain anything they will need to know that does not relate to the story. Once the story begins, it will kill the mood to break your 'presidium' by telling them something that would suggest that the world/town you created is false. Remember, you want your guests to feel like they are actually participating in a real adventure. Answer any and all questions they may have at this time as well.

Well, your guests understand as much as they can at this point and you are ready to send them on their way. You have your Preshow portion and watch as your teams begin their quest. What now?

THE QUEST BEGINS…

As soon as your guests have all entered the playing area (or gotten in their cars, if a car rally), it is your time to make 'your rounds.' By this, I mean walking the playing area, stopping by each character. There is no need to break the presidium by talking to the characters (unless it is imperative that you do so.) Simply make eye contact with every character. If there is a problem, they will let you know with their eyes. As you walk around, you want to seem invisible. If all goes well, you will not need to speak to any character. Once you've completed one 'round,'  make another, making eye contact with each character. Continue this process for the duration of the quest.

THINGS TO LOOK OUT FOR

As you are making your rounds, enjoying yourself far beyond your expectations, there are a few things to look out for.

A hole in the quest. This single presence can bring about more panic than any other problem. What is a hole? A hole is when, despite the incredible amount of effort you put into designing your quest, there is a disconnection somewhere. For example, let us say a team must collect three separate objects. But you have forgotten to include the third item on the list when you were typing them out. What do you do? If you do not do anything, the teams will not know about the third item (that was omitted from their list) and they will not have a chance in Hades to complete their quest. You might pull the character that gives them the list aside and explain your error. The character can either then add the item to the list by hand, as he passes the clue out, or verbally mention it to the teams. By the time the event happens, you will be so familiar with your storyline and characters that you should be able to repair any holes that might appear.

How do you detect holes? As you make your rounds, pay attention to what the teams are talking about. Watch teams as they complete different tasks. If you have a certain area that teams can only get to if they have completed certain tasks correctly, and it remains empty for an unusual amount of time, do a little backtracking to make sure that you have made it possible for them to get there.

Be aware of any cheating. The ultimate goal for the evening is for your guests to enjoy themselves. You are not going to want to play 'Cheater Gestapo' any more than they are going to want you to. However, it is still good to keep an eye out for any team that could be potentially making it impossible for other teams to finish.

Be aware of the timing. In Part III, you will learn how to create a timeline for your quest. By a certain time, you can expect that a certain number of teams will have achieved a certain position in their adventure. By a certain time you have planned on, your teams should begin coming in from completing their adventure.

What if the timing is not going as planned? If your guests are taking longer to complete their mission than you had planned, there is nothing wrong with modifying your quest. You might need to tell a couple key characters to freely give out certain information and minimize the amount of time the teams are talking to the characters. To take more time off your quest will rely heavily on the actual quest itself. After you have created your quest, note some ways to speed things up if there's a timing problem.

What if the opposite occurs? What if teams are completing their tasks much quicker than you had anticipated? This is easier to fix. Simply mention to all your characters to talk to the teams more. This should not be a problem for your actors as long as you have given them good characters to work with.

\

WRAPPING THINGS UP

Well, the last team has come in and all your guests are raving about how much fun they had. As soon as you are able to, it is a good idea to announce the winning team. In Part II under 'Post show', I have given several ideas on how to creatively end your quest. You might give a special award to the team chosen by the actors. The criteria might be how well the team interacted with the characters. Once the quest is over, I have found that the guests get a big kick out of talking to the actors out of character. It gives them a chance to tell the actors what a great job they did.

Now you are ready for a real good night's sleep. Be prepared, though, because it is not over yet….remember, your guests are going to be talking about this event months, even years later!!!

CHAPTER 7

Different Events

Okay, so, you are excited about designing your first quest, but what form will it take?

The Small Group Party

The ultimate goal is that your guests enjoy themselves. Chances are your guests are people you know fairly well, perhaps even intimately. You can design your quest around what you feel would go over best based on the personalities, abilities, and interests of these guests. Because your guests are close to you, it might seem more 'believable' if you have one of your characters introduce the quest in character rather than you.

The Fund-raiser

In my experience, there have been two major different ways to earn money through providing a quest. One is to plan the event and then sell tickets. The actual amount of the tickets varies greatly on the time and energy you have put into designing the quest. Prizes could be offered to the winning team(s). For one event, every team of four had an entrance fee of ten dollars ($2.50 each member). The winning team won 25% of the proceeds. There were 160 participants, so each member of the winning team won $25.00 while the event proceeds were $300 (not including about $30 spent on minor expenses.) This worked great for high school students because of the low cost to participate. However, one could easily charge $20 per person (include some food) and the numbers would greatly change ($200 per person and $1100 for the fund-raiser!) Another way to offer a prize is to have a local merchant donate a prize in exchange for some form of advertising. If your prize coincided with your theme, it would be easy to work the advertising in with the quest. Travel prizes work great for most themes.

A second approach to raising money is planning an overall themed event and charging tickets to come to that. For instance, you could plan a Charles Dickens Christmas dinner with musical entertainment and the like (similar to a Madrigal Dinner) and then provide the quest sometime during the event. Again, with such a wide variety of themes available, there should be no difficulty in coming up with a multitude of ideas for providing a great themed event to surround your quest.

The Progressive Dinner

Combining a quest with the format of a Progressive Dinner can be very challenging if it is your first time. The tricky part to manage is all your guests arriving at the same place at the same time. The result is having a line-up of your guests waiting for their turn to talk to a character or some other activity. The way to get around this is to split the activities and have different guests complete different tasks in different orders. This can get very tricky. The Progressive Dinner is manageable on a simple level only. Many of the suggestions in this book may not apply. They would either cause too much congestion/traffic in-between your stops or would take your guests four hours to complete their quest (neither option is very desirable).

The Car Rally

The car rally can be a very exciting option for a quest. First, make sure your guests are able to 'physically' handle completing their mission. It takes a lot of energy for your guests to get out of their car, walk (or run) to where they need to go, and then return to their car.

Another thing worth mentioning is it takes time away from your quest for your guests to drive from here to there. If you keep to the 55/75 minute rule, then you are stuck with not a lot of playing time if they spend a significant amount of time driving. The best way to see what I mean is to drive a probable path that you anticipate for your guests traveling in order to complete your quest. You will probably spend a lot more time driving than you first realized. Car rallies can be great, but not if you plan one that will take longer than an hour or so. Trust me, all that driving can really wear out even the most enthused adventurer!

A final thing to mention in planning a car rally is that it will be difficult for you to 'see it happening.' Even if you attempt to drive to the different stops to watch your guests enjoying themselves, you will still only catch 20% of the fun, at best. Additionally, if there is a problem, such as a hole, you will probably never know until you noticed that none of your guests has arrived at the final destination. For example, if you had a typo on a clue, there is no way to catch it, or fix it either.

The Haunted House

Haunted houses are perhaps one of the most fascinating parts of our modern day culture. Here we have perfectly sane people paying good money to enter an enclosed facility for the sole purpose of being scared. Even the smallest haunted house can be extremely successful, if done properly. A quest seems to be born for this kind of format. The reason is its originality and attempt to recreate reality. A great way to bill your event is to put this phrase in your sign "Anyone can shut their eyes and escape from a haunted house, but who has the guts to voluntarily stay inside and explore!" In *Nosferatu*, the guests were challenged not to find their way out of town, but to stay in town (no matter how scared they got) until their task was finished. Talk about something new and exciting to do for Halloween!

If you are holding the event on Halloween, you might need to arrange to have groups enter in shifts. It is difficult, sometimes, to know exactly how many people will want to participate. It would be a small disaster if you have 40 teams enter a quest that was only prepared for 15. Always know how many teams are inside at any given time. When one team exits, allow a new one to enter.

Social Organization Event

Social Organization Events range from under 100 participants to over a thousand. Although this book cannot tackle the complications of handling groups that large, many of the principles discussed can be

applied. Groups of that size would be another book all together…
hmmm…perhaps I have something there.

For an Individual

This format can be the simplest as well as the most involved…at the
same time it takes a different perspective. So many more possibilities
are available when you do not have to allow for more than one
person/team going on the event. Let me explain.

As before mentioned, I designed a quest for my brother's high school
graduation where he got to be Bruce Wayne over the course of a week.
Because it was only him, I was able to do the following (and much
more) during that week as part of his Batman adventure:
- He was able to meet Salina Kyle, Cat Woman's alter ego,
  as Bruce Wayne, for lunch.
- He received a strange phone call from one of the Riddler's
  ex-henchmen to arrange a meeting.
- I actually found a stunt man from the third Batman movie
  (just got lucky) who agreed to follow my brother around
  one day while he searched for clues. He blocked my
  brother's car in a parking lot and threatened my brother
  (calling him Bruce Wayne the entire time) to drop the case.

Follow where I am going? You can get down right personal. It makes
for an unforgettable experience. With the format, the participant can
receive phone calls, be followed, and can receive mail, to name just a
few ideas. My brother, being a huge Batman fan, will never forget that
graduation nor his once in a lifetime experience being Bruce Wayne.

PART II

Ideas, Ideas, and more Ideas!

In Part I, I have detailed the specifics of what a quest is and advice on how to create and organize one. Now I would like to introduce the frosting - those delicious ideas that will push your event to an even greater level.

CHAPTER 8

Decorating Your Quest

When it comes to setting the mood or atmosphere, no sense is more crucial than sight. No matter what theme you choose, there are many inexpensive ways to create the proper setting. Although eventually through my business I was able to acquire period props and costumes to aid in  this task, for most of my years creating quests I was left with only what was in my garage or what I could borrow from friends – which wasn't a lot. In just about every metropolitan area, you can find a prop warehouse, a company that will rent out props and set pieces for just about any theme. My experience, however, proves that they overcharge and the product is not always in the best shape.

Here are several ideas for decorating your playing area.

Lighting

Many things can be done with lighting. A lack of light is a good place to start. Sometimes there are things you DO NOT want to be seen. Simply make sure that these areas are as dimly lit as possible. Rooms lit dimly or by candlelight give a mysterious feel that is quite effective in transforming a familiar room into an unfamiliar one.

You can change the color of the lighting by buying different colored light bulbs from home furnishing stores. Usually they are only a few bucks. This can be very effective if you want to create the feeling of a forest, but you do not have access to many plants. The trick is to have a single lamp with a green light bulb in the room. At the entrance to the room, put any and all plants you can get your hands on (even if only a couple). Play the game of first impressions. If the threshold to the room is lined with plants, the guests will associate the contents of the room with plants as well. Likewise, a red light would work well for a vampire's den. Perhaps a purple light would work best to show the inside of a cave or tunnel.

A word about purple lights (also know as 'black lighting'). At stage and lighting stores, you can purchase glow in the dark paint (these are also obviously found online.) I built a town sign that I used for all my vampire themed quests. It was merely some rotted, old wood nailed together. What made it great was that I used red, black-lighting paint to write the words of the sign. It was posted with a black light below it, causing the red letters to glow, at the entrance to the town. It gave a wonderfully eerie first impression.

Costumes

Costumes can be a tough problem, depending on your theme. Sometimes I have chosen a theme based on the costumes I had available to me. A great source, where you can get lucky sometimes, is asking around to friends you know. Everyone has a few costume pieces from past talent shows and Halloween parties packed away in their garage. It just takes a little effort on the phone as you ask those you know what they would be willing to let you borrow. Of course, you can always rent costumes from costume shops, but costume expenses can run up quickly. If you choose to go with the costume shops, call around first. You would be surprised how each shop can differ in price. Sometimes, I have been lucky finding costume pieces at thrift and second-hand stores (especially around the end of summer when they are getting ready for Halloween).

As an added note, you might want to consider asking your guests to come in appropriate costume. This can enhance the mood if the teams can look around and see that everyone is dressed according to the theme. The only drawback is that the characters may not stick out as well as you might like. Some of the guests could show up with similar costumes to one your characters. A case in point was when I held my quest for the Holy Grail and the teams were informed to find Merlin. Well, about five guests that night were in a Merlin costume. It caused confusion for the teams and especially for the poor Merlins in the crowd.

What about you? Should you be in costume? Well, if your guests are, then you should be as well. If your guests are not, then I guess you have the option. Just make sure that if you do choose to be in costume, it will not inhibit your movement. The last thing you want to worry about is whether or not your seven-foot Minion costume will fit through the door jams as you make your rounds.

Fabric

It is amazing what a little fabric and creativity can do for creating a themed setting. It might be helpful to scout around your area for discount fabric stores. Find the cheapest material you can find, but with a pattern that you can use. For example, I had a character that was dressed as a French aristocrat sitting in her bedroom writing in a diary. It took enough time and money to have her costume look right that I had nothing left for her surroundings. As a result, I bought some ornate fabric that I draped behind her making fake curtains. I took some remaining fabric and made a small tablecloth for where she was sitting. It cost me only a few dollars, but it looked fantastic. This can be done for just about any theme.

Cardboard

Stacked boxes can do wonders for creating a structure for a room. Suppose you want to split a room in half. Simply stack boxes on top of each other and then use the drapery suggestions as described above or paint them to look like the walls of an Egyptian temple or pirate ship. Additionally, if you can manage to transport one, refrigerator boxes make terrific walls. Simply cut the top, bottom, and the seam on one side and you have a four-partitioned wall that can be folded and moved to suit any spacing needs.

A secret tip I learned was to find a small company that deals in insulation. The insulation is wrapped around large rolls of cardboard (like a seven foot tall toilet paper roll). These are often thrown out or recycled. I have been known to obtain a few of these and paint them to look like pillars of a temple. They looked fantastic!

Utilize natural surroundings as much as possible. If a scene needs to take place in a jungle, do your best to have your teams go outside. You can utilize parks in this same way. Get to know your playing area well enough so you can utilize each area to its fullest potential.

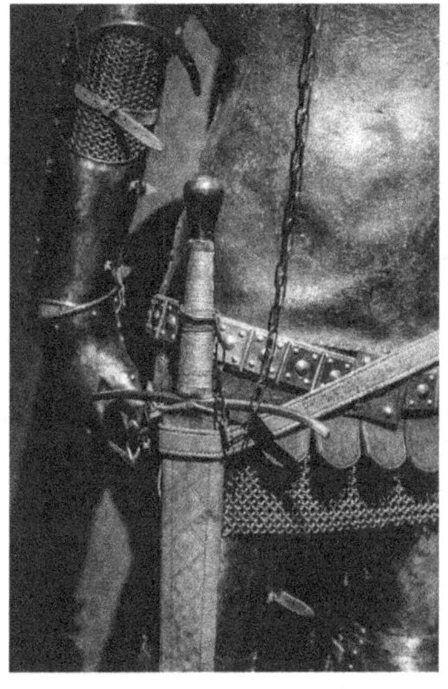

Final notes on decorating. In our zeal and unbridled creativity, there can be the temptation to use some decoration that we have available, but may be better left out. Remember, if it will not enhance your theme, it will detract from it and could even look out of place.

When deciding on how to decorate your quest event, keep in mind that you are trying to transport your guests to an exciting, new place. One of my hostesses got excited about decorating her home according to the pirate themed quest she was planning. She bought black streamers as well as balloons, plates and cups, all with Jolly Roger flags imprinted on them. Once the quest began, she regretted buying all that she had bought. She explained to me that if she had the chance to do it over, she would have bought some cheap wooden cups, some metal pie plates, and lots of fishing nets. Her balloons and streamers gave the impression to her guests that the quest she had planned would be nothing more than a 'little game' and her guests were tempted to treat it as such.

You do not have to decorate the entire playing area with the same intensity. If there is a stop or location that your guests will be spending more time at, it might be a good idea to give this location a little more attention in the decorating department. The opposite is also true.

The Portal

A concept worth discussing before leaving the topic of decorating is the Portal. The Portal area I am referring to is the actual threshold that your guests will cross before entering the playing area. This may be a front door, a hallway, or some other form, depending on your playing area. I always decorate the Portal with more attention. You see, I want my guests to leave 'their world' behind and step into 'my world.' I am helping them step into 'this new world' when I give them a specific, visual doorway. If they are going back in time, I might decorate the Portal with fake pipes and cardboard boxes to replicate a time machine. In a pirate theme, I might have the guests walk down a boarding plank from a makeshift side of a ship to the playing area. Of course, rarely would I ever have access to the actual side of a ship to use just for the Portal, you'd be surprised how far a little creativity and resourcefulness will take you.

CHAPTER 9

Sound

Sound can be a powerful tool when creating atmosphere for a particular scene. The budget may be is tight, but you do not need to compromise the effect. Here are some different, creative uses of sound.

One option is to have music in the background of the entire playing area. This can easily be achieved if the entire quest is contained within a house, but would require a nicer sound system if your location is a large gymnasium or other such facility. What music should you play? This is another time when you get to be extra creative. We have to look at the theme you have chosen. WHERE is your quest being held? Is it in the Caribbean? Is it in the south of France? Is it in the jungles of Africa? In addition, you need to ask yourself WHEN is your quest? Is it taking place 5000 years ago in Egypt, in 17th century Germany, or last week in New York City? These will all affect your choice in background music. Check into soundtracks from movies of the same theme or ethnic music from your quest's geographical area. Music without lyrics is always preferred to those with. You want the background music to be just that, background music. Let it accentuate your environment, not make itself noticeable. Additionally, make sure your music is not contradictory to the action. By this, I mean it would not be the wisest choice to play a slow, classical piano concerto if the teams are racing to diffuse a bomb that is about to blow up the city!

Likewise, be mindful of the volume. It may be tempting to pump up the volume, particularly if you are especially proud of the music you chose. Do not give in, though. Your guests are going to be doing a lot of talking and thinking. Make sure your environment is conducive to such.

A bit on technology. Not all of us have access to a great sound system. Perhaps your entire quest will be outside where you will not even have access to a power source. As a rule of thumb, I only include sound if I am able to do so in a non-obtrusive way. I only use it if it supports the scene. I am always asking myself "Is this sound distracting?" Sometimes the music you choose will not be distracting, but the quality of the sound will. If this is the case, you might want to consider leaving it out. Also, make sure that the music loops in some way. It would break the mood if your guests heard a disruption in the background music. Do your best to avoid this from happening.

It is possible to have separate music for different scenes. When I held an Indiana Jones themed quest for some friends, I used separate music for each scene. When the teams met Lao Che, a Chinese art collector, traditional Chinese music played softly in the background. When they confronted Hitler while he sat behind his desk in Berlin, loud German folk music, reminiscent of Nazi rallies, played behind him. Always remember to choose music that accentuates not only the scene, but the action as well. Do not play fast, marching music if the scene has a character sleeping in bed. Additionally, make sure the sound sources do not conflict with each other. Stand at each scene and make sure you are not able to hear the sounds coming from another scene (unless it's a deliberate choice to do so).

Sometimes music would be entirely inappropriate. Perhaps your quest is located in the jungles of Africa. It might break the mood if you played music. After all, where would it be coming from (save a distant beating of a jungle drum)? Terrific compilations of  sound effects can be found with every animal sound imaginable. Likewise, every weather condition can be replicated such as snowstorms, rain showers, even crashing waves. Is your quest in the 'urban jungle?' Well, how about police sirens and trains storming by?

When using these types of sounds, it is best to have some silent intervals between them.

It is possible to combine music with sound effects. Perhaps your quest takes place at a Caribbean pirate port. Have 17th century calliope music playing with an occasional sea gull sound, a crash of lighting or canon shot for further fun and excitement. Explore all your possibilities and have fun with it! Just about every sound can be found online!

CHAPTER 10

Clues and Maps

CLUES

No matter what theme you choose, chances are you will be giving your guests several different pieces of paper. They might be old maps, official letters from Scotland Yard, or friendly notes from a French aristocrat. The following  is a compilation of tricks and tips for turning your clues into impressive souvenirs your guests will want to keep to remember the event.

FONTS

Fonts, or actual design/script of the letters, can be a lot of fun to work with and consider when creating your written materials – and literally 1000's of fonts can be found online, including handwriting fonts. Which font(s) you choose will obviously very much depend on WHO created the document. Notice how I did NOT say depending on your theme. You see, you might have two different pirate documents – one written by a Spanish pirate and the other written by French aristocrat. Their writing styles would be very different (one likely being more educated than the other as well as the cultural differences.) These might seem like small details but it's these details that will make your adventure feel more real, even if only subliminally. This detail is especially important if the teams will be encountering more than one document from the same person (to keep their writing not only accurate, but consistent.)

For reference, do searches online for historical documents from your time period and geographical location/country within your theme. You'll be able to see not only the style of fonts that were used, but also placement on the paper (did they use heavy margins or does the writing extend to the edge of the paper?) and the actual size of the font itself. It may seem like a lot of trouble to go through for a piece of paper that will just get thrown away, right? Wrong. When I go through that much trouble, not only does it say WOW to my guests, but I've found these pieces of paper never make it to the trash. Your guests will end up keeping the clues as mementos of the evening. I have heard stories of guests taking the clues to the office on the following Monday, showing their coworkers the great time they had at the party!

What if the character isn't English speaking per se?…which brings us next to…

LANGUAGES

It is quite possible that your quest will take your guests to some other part of the world. A great way to give the feel of being in a foreign country is through language. Now, don't start stressing if you don't speak a lick of any language other than English. I am only talking about a word here and there. Thanks to the Internet and Google Translate, you can translate just about any word or phrase into any other language.

A terrific way to incorporate a foreign language into your quest is to have the participants translate some as part of their adventure. Perhaps they find a note in a tavern in France and it is written entirely in French. Maybe they find a secret World War II note and must translate it to thwart a secret invasion. No matter what the clue might reveal or what the language is, make sure you give the teams a simple way of translating it. Perhaps, as part of their 'start up' package, you give them a sheet of 50 useful words in the foreign language at hand. In your clue, only use a portion of the words that you provide on your translation sheet. Otherwise, if all the words on your translation sheet could be used to make a sentence or two, clever teams may play around with the words to guess a message and jump way ahead of where you had intended them to go.

ANTIQUING YOUR CLUES

Because the majority of the themes I have worked with have been of a historical nature, it became necessary to come up with several different ways of aging the paper my clues are printed on. Sometimes I have needed paper to look hundreds (or even thousands) of years old and other times I have needed official government paper issued by NASA dating back to last week.

If you want your paper to look old, there are several things you can do. We offer several different themes of blank paper in our Amazon Store. Each page is hand aged so that it not only looks old, it feels old. Themes include everything from pirates to ancient Egypt. However, there are also methods that you can do at your own home. Let us begin with the kind of paper you choose. There are several different kinds of parchment paper you can purchase. If you have a paper supply store near you, you will find you can save a lot by going there. Copy service centers sell them as well, but it is more expensive when you buy them by the individual sheet. Additionally, these centers will discount your copy prices if you bring in your own paper. Of course, ordering specialty paper online is always an option…however it can be difficult to really get a feel for the paper when it's only an image on the screen.

Here's a process we developed for aging paper to create a 'crunchy' or even brittle effect. Although it can be time consuming, the result can be well worth the time spent. For example, when aging a pirate map, once I have the map image copied onto the standard stock white copy paper (the cheaper the paper, the better), I give it a crispy, water soaked feel by treating it in the following way. Preheat a standard kitchen oven to BROIL. Please do not confuse this with the BROILER of a gas oven. Place an old, flat cookie sheet on the top rack of the oven. With any can of cheap aerosol laundry spray starch, spray a single piece of paper and quickly lay it flat on the hot cookie sheet you have in the hot oven. Keep a close eye on the paper as the oven does its work. Initially, the paper will probably begin to curl and then finally flatten again. As it flattens, keep your eye on it. The brown discoloring can happen rather quickly. Once the paper is the desired color, remove the paper from the cookie sheet with an oven mitt and repeat the previous steps until you have aged all your maps and clues. The process gives the paper a stiffer effect, like paper that was once soaked in water and then left out in the sun to dry. To further the effect, leave the paper in the oven longer. The paper will get darker, however the image should still be readable. Due to the prolonged time in the oven, the paper will become extremely brittle. Now, your guests will have to make sure they take extra care of the map/clue or else it will break into several pieces!

BURNING PAPER

Once you've treated/antiqued your paper, try burning the edges. Sometimes burning off a mere corner is enough. Other times, extensive burning might be the only way to achieve the look you want. Either way, follow these helpful steps to ensure success. First off, make sure that you are in a safe, well-ventilated place away from flammable materials. Also, make sure you are safe from any breezes. The best flame source is a small votive candle. They are stable and inexpensive. Place the candle on a small plate or piece of cardboard before lighting it. This will catch all the melted wax these candles are notorious for. Holding the paper horizontally over the flame, bring it closer until the edge barely ignites. Let the paper burn slowly until you have reached either the desired burn or the flame is beginning to get out of control. It is better to do several small controlled burns, than one out of control one. At this time, sandwich the paper in between an old, folded over towel and pat it down until there are NO BRIGHT ORANGE CINDERS on the edge of the paper. Different papers have different chemicals. Some paper, unless you completely blot them as described, will continue burning very slowly, consuming the whole sheet if you allow it. Repeat this process until you have achieved the desired look. For the best results, let the paper burn unevenly. As a fun idea, you might want to put a small note on your maps saying something like "To quickly find the treasure, go to…" and then burn that last part off. The effect is that the map once had the answer the teams will be looking for, but it was burned off.

For another interesting effect, try lowering the paper upon the flame vertically. The flames will create black burning streaks, rising up the edge of the paper. Although tricky, it produces some great results.

SAFETY TIP!!! DO NOT ROLL THE PAPER WHEN BURNING THE EDGES!!! The funnel you create can cause fire to shoot up inside the tube, possibly burning your hands or face.

It is also possible to burn a small (or large) hole in the MIDDLE of the paper.   First tear or cut out the desired hole SMALLER than you'd like, but as close to the desired shape as possible. Look over the candle directly from above as you lower your hole in the paper onto the flame. Use the bright light of the flame as it shows itself through the thin paper as a guide. Place the flame directly under where you want the hole to be and burn the interior edges as described above. This is a handy tool if for some reason you've made a mistake on your document and don't want to create a new one. It's the treasure hunters way of 'deleting' the text.

A final note when dealing with burning paper…it can be very messy. The ashes that burn off tend to make a black mess In addition, your paper will now be equally as messy (especially around the edges). You might want run a towel along all the burnt edges to scrape or break off any pieces that are still attached. Perhaps not, though. If you are going for the extremely brittle approach as previously described, you may want to leave all the burnt ashes still attached to your edges.

Once you have your paper, you can take things a step further. Try treating the envelope. You might want to burn a corner off the envelope. A neat trick, though it requires spending a little money, is to go to a craft store and purchase a small wax sealer. They are great fun to use and really make your piece look from another time.

MAKING IT LOOK OFFICIAL

There are times when you will need a clue to look official. It may need to appear as though it was an official IRS document or an invoice from the ACME Rubber Chicken Factory.

Sometimes, you can be clever enough with some letterhead creations. Countless images can be found online and I've found it to be a lot of fun to create all different types of paper materials. Creating letterhead, business cards for your characters, stationary, fake government documents – all will help your guests get into the story!

Here are some other ideas for sprucing up your envelopes. I created a quest where the participants began with a letter mailed from a professor who was last seen in the jungles of Africa. I made envelopes for the letters that looked like they came from Africa. First of all, I found some odd shaped envelopes at a stationary supply store, ones that didn't look like the normal business size or shape that we all readily recognize here in the US. Secondly, I MADE an image of a stamp of an elephant using a computer graphics program. I then ran the envelopes through the printer and printed the stamp image in the upper right corner. Then, using my handy graphics program again, I made a squiggle line design with the circular words of the date and made up Congo village. The overall effect was as though the letter had been 'post-marked' by the post office in Africa with the date and location of my choice. Another great idea is to buy some cancelled stamps from different countries online. They can be VERY inexpensive and will look AMAZING on your envelopes

Sometimes your clue will need to look like an application that has been filled out, such as a police report. I once created a police filing cabinet with certain pieces of paper from a file to steal. The paper was a police form filled out about a specific case. It looked great. I created a blank form using Microsoft Word and included some letterhead techniques as described above. Now you can also change the font to include the writing of the person who FILLED OUT the form, but I've found that that looks a bit overly formatted and fake. For a GREAT look, ask around to see if someone has an old typewriter (I know, I know…but ask around anyway.) Once I printed the blank form, I took it to a typewriter and typed in the needed information. When you use an actual typewriter, you get the odd spacing of lines. The typewriter line spacing won't evenly match up with the ones on the form (as they never do…). The results were very effective!

MAPS

No matter where your storyline takes place, it takes place *somewhere.* That *somewhere* could be someplace real, like Port Royal in the Caribbean, or someplace fictitious like the pirate port of El Diablo (the town I made up for

Dark Fortune). By providing a physical map for your guests to hold onto and use, they will be able to mentally place themselves into your world.

Why reinvent the wheel? You can find countless images of old maps online. In a graphic program you can then insert your own words on top of the map image, including your own city/village names or words of caution (whatever you need as part of your adventure

Sometimes your map will already have writing on it and applying your own handwritten messages might make it look awkward. Use the ideas from the Font section to see how you can find lettering that would match what's already on your map. This can be a handy trick, especially if you have a lot of writing to put on your map. Sometimes you are left with no other alternative but to make your own map from scratch. Just make sure to use a dark marker that will reproduce well on a copy machine.

SUGGESTIONS FOR HOW TO GIVE A MAP

The following lists several ways to supply your teams with a map, other than simply providing them with it when you explain the rules.

- They could earn it. Perhaps if they meet a cartographer in town they could perform a favor for him in exchange for a map of their choice.
- They could buy it. Before the quest begins you could supply each team with some fake money or jewels to use

for bartering. Alternatively, you could have the teams WORK for their money, getting a job of some sort.

- They could find it. Perhaps they might find one as in Chapter 11's example of rummaging through a university professor's desk.

- They could steal it. The teams must be creative on how to distract the original owner of the map long enough to snatch it. As an amusing anecdote, I once held a pirate quest for 20 graduating eighth graders. Each team needed to steal a piece of a map from an aristocratic woman. She used the map piece (she had several, one for each team) as a bookmark for the book she was reading. As the young teams spoke to her, she kept her hands on the book at all times. She was not going to make it easy for them. At one point in the quest, she (the actress) came running up to me, leaving her station (it took place within a country club clubhouse) with a concerned look on her face. She frantically asked me what the emergency was. I, a bit confused, said "What emergency?" She then replied "Didn't you just send them over to get me to…Oh my gosh!" And with that she ran back to her station, and sure enough those eighth graders who told her that I needed to speak to her stole her bookmark map piece. The actress laughed and said that she felt swindled.

- Any combination of the above, especially if your map is in several different pieces.

CHAPTER 11
Characters Without Actors

Sometimes, even though you have tried your darndest, you still are not going to be able to find enough volunteers to play characters in your quest. You still want to stick to your storyline, so what do you do?

Voice Recordings

This single tool can solve 95% of your lack of volunteer dilemmas. Of course, it is much more exciting for your participants if they can meet your characters face to face, it IS possible to conduct an entire quest with a number of laptops/phones/music players. Let me give an example of one use. Once I created a dungeon out of a hallway of closed doors. I took black painted PVC pipes and propped them vertically in the door jams of each closed door, creating a prison-cell look. I then made several voice tapes on continuous audio cassettes of different prisoners in their cells (yep…audio cassettes…that's how long I've been creating these!) I put a different tape and tape recorder behind each of the closed cell doors. One cell had two prisoners arguing over food, another was praying for deliverance, and a third was mumbling out of delirium. The quest participants had needed only to listen to the mumbler for a few minutes before they heard him ramble on about some information they needed. Even though there wasn't a single living soul behind any of those doors, the participants would have sworn that it was a 'full house.'

Playing a recorded voice behind a closed door can be used in a great number of ways to solve your low volunteer count. The participants might listen to an argument between two characters. They might eavesdrop on a private phone conversation. They might simply hear sounds of someone sleeping. Even if you have plenty of volunteers to play all your characters, inserting one of these little tricks could bring some nice variety to your tasks.

Another use of the voice recording is to play a recording of a mock radio station or war communicator. Participants will have to listen to your 'radio program' in order to get the needed information. This would also work if you placed the speakers behind or inside a makeshift wartime communicator/radio. The voice could be full of static as though someone were trying to communicate from a battlefield.

Leave A Note

Try assigning the task of meeting a certain character at a specific time. However, once the teams would go to meet him or her, they would find that the character had gone, but left a message (either to the teams if they had a scheduled meeting, or to someone else where the teams get to be nosy and read someone else's message). Either way, you would have inserted the presence of another character without an actor.

You can also leave behind a piece of information that is NOT in the form of a note. Once I had teams meet a research professor at his office. Once they got there, though, they had found he had left for a couple of hours, but left the door unlocked. Teams then went in and perused through the professor's papers and books, looking for the information they needed.

Mail

Depending on the size of the event and nature of the guests, it might be possible to mail the participants a piece of information beforehand. This is a great way to spark enthusiasm for the event in the few days before. This also helps to begin the story BEFORE the actual quest begins. When I've designed and planned a quest for an individual, I almost always mail them something beforehand…mostly because who doesn't love to get a fun piece of mail!?

Phones

As I mentioned in Chapter 7, you could have a single participant receive a phone call as part of the quest. However, how could you use the phone when you have multiple teams? Do what I do and have the participants call a given phone number. You could handle this in one

of two ways. First, you could have someone on the other end of the line speaking to the teams in character (perhaps someone who couldn't be a volunteer because they couldn't find a babysitter for their kids). Secondly, you could change the message on the phone to give the needed information (like where to find the character because he is on vacation…)

The fact that nearly every person has their own cell phone in today's world adds more opportunities for characters than I ever had 30 years ago when I first began creating quests. Assuming your theme allowed for the use of cell phones (any theme in present day such as a search for Bigfoot or perhaps world espionage), you can have multiple volunteers play characters without even showing up to your event. All they would need to do is answer their phones or return a text during a certain time period (the time interval of your quest) as a certain character. I've used this VERY often because it's easy and effective. A quick, fun anecdote: For my youngest son's 18th birthday I set up a quest for him and a couple of his friends to hunt for a werewolf in the city (before he transformed.) It was during a full moon and the three only had a couple of hours to find him. At one point they were given a phone number of another werewolf, a friend to the one they were hunting for. Their goal was to call him and to persuade him to offer information that might help them find his friend. He was able to give some information (not too much)…but then began making horrible noises over the phone as though he were transforming himself (after all, it WAS a full moon.) It was very effective and it was great watching my son's and his friends' faces turn white as they heard the screams and eventually howling on the other end of the phone after speaking to man for a few minutes. It only took a few minutes out of my friend's evening to play the part and he had a blast doing it!

These are just a few ways to incorporate the feeling of live characters without having them. There are many more ways to accomplish this, though. Let your imagination guide you as you explore your theme.

CHAPTER 12

Preshow and Post show

PRESHOW

The Preshow, as I have come to call it, is any part of your quest that happens after your guests arrive but before they begin the adventure. It is any creative way you 'kick off' your adventure, giving your guests an immediate and desperate need to go on your 
quest. In *In Search of the Holy Grail*, King Arthur called everyone in his kingdom together (all the guests at the party) to announce that the Holy Grail would be presented. Once everyone was together and he had their attention, he began to say a few words about the grail itself and finally called out "And now, I present the Holy Grail!" However, nothing happened. The guests began to look around at each other and waited for something to happen. Arthur said once more "I said, I present to you all, The Holy Grail!" Still nothing. Finally, from a door behind everyone, came rushing in a beaten up knight yelling at the top of his lungs "The Grail has been stolen!" He then fought his way through the crowd to announce to everyone how Morgana the Sorceress has stolen the Grail and that he was the only one that survived to tell the tale. Arthur then made a plea to all his subjects to join together to help find the grail. The teams (who had already been explained the rules) got into their groups and began their adventure.

There are many creative things that can be done during this time, all of which can add excitement and anticipation for your guests in what they are about to participate in. In *Nosferatu*, I stood before all the guests to explain the rules and what was about to happen. Toward the end of this part, some of the characters from the town (those they would meet later) began spreading out among the guests. In my storyline, the townspeople had but all been killed off, save a few, by vampires. Once the rules were explained, one of the townspeople shouted out (interrupting me) "Enough talk!" Then another piped in "Who will save our children!" Then, the rest of the townspeople joined in, holding up rakes and pitchforks, as though a mob was being incited (like in the old Frankenstein movie). The guests felt as though they were a part of an angry village mob in an old black and white movie going to hunt down 'the monsters.'

Let me first suggest that you do not begin any part of your Preshow until after you have gathered everyone together to explain the rules (unless you have come up with a clever way to explain the rules as part of your Preshow.) This is because you do not want to have a break in *presidium*. Presidium is a theater term for when the actors step out of character and give information to the audience. It breaks the illusion of the story being told. Once the rules are over and the preshow begins, it is best not to go back, but rather to tread on until the adventure begins. Think of the preshow as the first scene of your movie. It would be distracting to stop your movie once it has begun. Once your movie starts, its best to let it go (unless of course you have no other choice.)

However, I *have* been known to break this rule. For a quest I performed at a private Halloween party, I stationed ghosts throughout the large house, all making commotion every now and again, but never engaging any of the guests. For the first hour or so, the guests were merely aware of, and very amused by, these 'party crashers' and left them to themselves. Once the quest was about to begin, I (whom stayed out of sight until this point) rang the front doorbell and came in uniform as a paranormal exterminator. I walked around with bogus gadgets taking 'readings' of all kinds and passed around my business cards to the guests. Once I had everyone's attention, I pulled all the guests together in a large room and explained to them I needed everyone's help in ridding the estate of the ghosts. The guests then got in groups of four and began exploring the house, finding many more ghosts than they originally thought, and had a fantastic time trying to learn how to get rid of each one.

In the above example, I had part of the Preshow (the part when I came in character and set the stage for what the guests would be doing) start earlier (when a couple of the ghosts were visible, yet minding their own business.) In this particular quest, I was

able to have a part of the action begin way before the teams began the adventure because I worked the rules of play INTO the Preshow. Most of the time this is very difficult and I would suggest waiting to start your preshow activities AFTER you have explained the rules.

When coming up with a Preshow, there are certain things that I always keep in mind:

- As stated before, make sure that the rules and anything that your guests need to know are explained BEFOREHAND. Do not start the movie until you are sure that you will not have to interrupt it.
- If possible, try to work in one of the characters explaining the rules as part of the preshow. This may take a little extra brainpower because you will need to figure out a way to explain the rules as part of the adventure. However, it is great if you are able to do it.
- Make it dramatic. Create a sense of urgency. Make your guests feel as though there is an emergency at hand and that they are desperately needed to solve the problem. Start it off with a bang!
- Have everyone already in teams BEFORE the preshow begins. Make sure that these teams are standing/sitting together so that NO action will exist between the preshow and the moment the guests begin the adventure.

As a final note, it is a good idea to give the teams something to start with, what I call a starter packet. Will your teams need money for their journey? A map? A piece of a clue? It is perfectly fine to have your teams earn the money as part of their adventure and buy their own map in town. However, you might want to give SOMETHING to the teams as they begin. This way they will not feel like they are starting at ground zero. It is a good idea at this time to give them a copy of the rules. You can work this into your preshow. It would have been perfectly acceptable for Arthur to give some gold to the teams in the beginning to help them on their journey, and he did so.

POST SHOW

What I call the Post Show is the final resolution to your movie. By this time, all the teams have finished their adventure and are having a great time sharing their experiences with each other. Be sure to allow time for this at your event. You will find that they will have just as much fun talking about it afterward as they had going through it.

Often times, there is a winner of some kind to announce. There can be any number of categories:

- The team who completed the quest in the quickest amount of time.
- The team who completed the most within a certain amount of time. For example, in the ghost/Halloween party described in the Preshow section, I gave all the guests ONE hour to try and rid the house of as many ghosts as they could. Each team had a way of tracking how many ghosts they found and how many they actually exterminated. The first place team was not the one who finished first (for there were too many ghosts to rid in a single hour) but rather the one who rid the estate of the most.
- Best Player Award. This is a special award that is best judged by your actors and volunteers. This award should go to the team who 'gets into' the adventure the most, the team who is the most creative when talking to the actors. In the previous example from Nosferatu where teams had to get past the doctor to speak to the dying woman, one of the team members began to 'cry' when she was told of the dying Durrell by the doctor. She did this to convince the doctor that she and Durrell were actually sisters. The doctor thought this was clever and ushered the team in quickly. Typically, remember, the team who 'gets into it' the most, finishes the quickest.
- Create your own within the theme. If you have a Western themed quest and a major part of the action is gambling in

different saloons, perhaps an award can be given to the team who won the most amount of 'money' along the way. This will depend greatly on the theme you choose and the tasks you place before your teams.

Your Post show should be the single event that wraps up your entire storyline. It is the time when King Arthur presents the recovered Grail to his Kingdom. It is the time when all the townspeople come to celebrate the ridding of the vampires. It is the time for all the conflicts to be resolved. A way to do this is to have the character that launched the quest in the preshow come back and call up the first place team to thank them for 'saving the day.' King Arthur could knight the team for recovering the Grail. You see, ideally, ALL the teams were able to finish their adventure and recover the Grail, but only the first place team will get the public glory for it, with the characters thanking them.

When creating my Post show, I keep the following in mind:

- Are all my storylines and subplots resolved? If not, now would be the time to do it.
- Sometimes a great way to end it is to have ALL the characters throughout the entire quest up on stage at the time of thanking the team. It 'breaks the presidium' a bit, but it is kind of fun for the guests to see all the characters one last time, and to applaud them.
- Make sure ALL the teams have completed (or given up) their adventure first.

Even if you find that you do not have any time left at the end of your quest and no awards will be given, it is still highly advisable to pull everyone together one last time to allow one of the characters (if not all) to thank the guests for 'saving the day.'

CHAPTER 13

Food

 Before we begin talking about what type of food to serve, there are a few considerations to think about. First, remember that your guests will be moving around, perhaps at a quick pace, and doing some writing. I learned early on that food definitely inhibits the action of a quest. Your guests will have enough on their hands enjoying your adventure. Additionally, remember we all tend to be a bit sluggish right after we eat. Therefore, my experience has also proved that the best time to serve food is AFTER your quest is over, if you are serving food at all. However, you also want to make sure that your guests are not starving as they play, either. We all tend to be a little less patient and even down right cranky when we are hungry. Perhaps some light finger foods might be appropriate before the quest gets rolling. You decide. Of course, if you are clever enough, you could incorporate the eating of food into your quest, but I have not been able to think of a way to do this without the guests eating too fast for the sake of continuing their adventure. If you think of something, please write me and let me know what you came up with!

A second consideration is in regards to your theme. As in the example presented in the decoration section, make sure that your food choice is closer to what your characters would have eaten versus a meat loaf with the words of your theme written on it in ketchup. Once again, the Internet is a great place to find this information. It will be the difference of good and great.

Now, let us talk about what to actually serve. You have the opportunity to have a whole lot of fun being as creative as you want. Check cookbooks and the Internet to get recipes or create your own. Always remember to consider your guests, but push the boundaries whenever possible. Is your quest located in the jungles of Africa? At large food markets one can find alligator meat. Will your guests enjoy an adventure in the Wild Wild West? What about buffalo burgers? Remember that your guests will have just gone on an exciting adventure and have worked up a great appetite. Why not continue the adventure while they're eating?

Part III

Enough Already, Let's Get Started!

Hopefully by reading Parts I and II of this book you have at least some ideas about what kind of quest you would like to design. Perhaps you know you are going to plan a fundraiser with a specific theme, but have no idea where you are going to hold it. On the other hand, perhaps you have absolutely no idea whatsoever what you are going to do themewise, other than you would like to try planning a quest. Wherever you fit in at this point, I will meet you there because we are starting from the ground floor and working our way up. If you already have a few ideas of what you would like to do, then you are a bit ahead of the game and you will be able to breeze through a couple parts of this process.

Throughout this part of the book, please feel free to flip back through Parts I & II for ideas and suggestions. Those parts of the book were written so that when you were ready to begin designing, you would have reference material at your disposal.

As you go through Part III, please note Appendix A wherein I have included a worksheet to use as you read. Feel free to make copies first, and then begin writing directly on the worksheet.

WHO AND WHERE?

Probably before anything else, these two questions need to be asked… and answered. There are several initial decisions to be made when designing a quest, but these two are the most important to nail down first. Most of the other decisions that you will make will hinge on how you answer these two.

The WHO, here, is WHO are going to be the guests and HOW MANY are going to participate. A quest planned for one close friend would be handled differently than one for 100 strangers. At this time, write the approximate number of guests on the worksheet, Item 1.

Now you need to get a good idea on where you will be able to hold your quest, based on the guests you expect to come. You may not know exactly what parts of your location you will be using, but at least you will know what you will be working with. Enter this location also on Item 1.

FUNCTION AND LENGTH OF TIME

Now that you know who will be coming where, it is time to decide for what and how long.

In Chapter 7, I have detailed different types of events where you could insert a quest. It is important at this time to commit to one of them because it will affect your choice of theme, which is coming up. (Item 2)

How long will the quest last? If your quest is embedded in a tight schedule of other events during one evening, it is VERY important to know how long you have so that the schedule for the entire event is not thrown completely off. If the quest is the only activity and the event itself is centered around it, commit to a length of time for your entire event, then one for the quest. As a note, please be as specific as possible when deciding on your length of time. For instance, 55 minutes is better than 'an hour or so.' Insert this time length in Item 3. Later on in the quest designing, we will work more with the timing of the tasks. Right now, though, it is only important for you to know the beginning and ending times.

THEMES AND STORYLINES

Time to put your creative hat on. This is where the true fun begins. If by chance you have not decided on a theme yet, it is time to decide now. Included in Appendix B of this book you will find a list of over 50 themes and over 100 storylines/ missions. As mentioned earlier, although the list may be far from exhaustive, it does provide the themes with the widest public appeal. If not a single theme appeals to you, let the list get your creative juices flowing to come up with one of your own. Once you have decided on your theme, you need to decide on a mission, some overall goal your guests will need to accomplish. Enter these two on the worksheet, Items 4 & 5.

BRAINSTORMING AND RESEARCH

Take out a pad of paper and begin writing down all words and phrases that pertain to your theme. Items to include would be places/locations, people, technology, actions, nouns, anything and everything that comes to mind. Below I have supplied a sample list to the theme of an professor lost in a jungle:

rain forest	snakes	lions
river	Belgian Congo	waterfall
lost	native uprising	safari
hunting	bamboo huts	Zimbabwe
Nigeria	Africa	old map
tribal king	tiger traps	ransom note
alligators	ancient writing	vines
suspension bridges	university professor	animal attacks
quicksand	rhinoceros	elephants
malaria	giraffe	passports
spears	poison darts	headdress
booby traps	luggage	bats
caves	gorillas	savannah
canteen	pith helmet	rain
spiders	scorpion	wars

religious curses	diamonds	Victoria Falls
local language	hiking	shooting
wading in river	campfire	mosquitoes

Once you've thought of every word and phrase you can think of pertaining to your theme, put your list down. Come back to it in an hour and try again. Usually there will be a few more words or ideas you had not thought of.

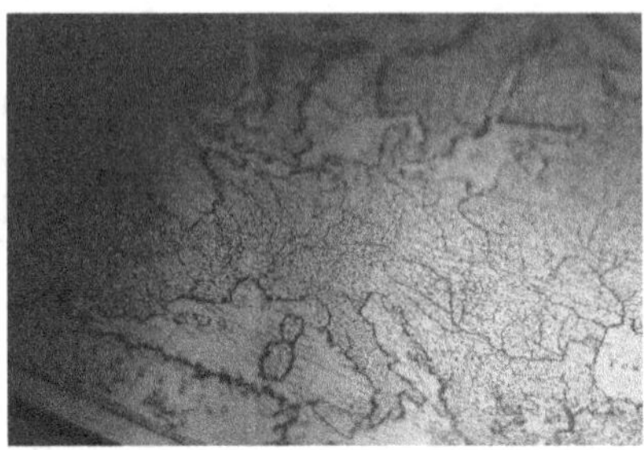

If you find that your list isn't as strong as you'd like it to be, here's a helpful trick: Go to the library and check out some children's books on your subject. If you enjoy reading, by all means, you can select some of the meatier, adult books. However, if you would like to cut to the chase and get to some quick ideas and information, you will find that children's non-fiction books work great. As you turn each page, (there are always a lot of pictures) more ideas and words will begin to come to mind. Do not turn a page until you have exhausted it of any new ideas. If your brain gets tired, then feel free to stop for a while. This process is very important and should not be taken lightly. You see, from these words and phrases will come 95% of your quest (you'll see how later.) Challenge yourself to come up with 100 words, then try coming up with another 50. Keep this up until you feel like you have more words and ideas than you could possibly fit into 100 quests.

I have been known to employ several other tricks in order to make sure that my list is complete. One is to ask other people to get involved (preferably people who aren't going to be coming to the event.) Other people will more than likely be able to come up with images you might not have thought of.

Movies are another great resource. Movies have been created on every theme out there. Notice how they set the mood. Notice the sets, props and costumes. Most importantly, though, catch those last few images that might have escaped your list. This process will not only help you strengthen your list, but it will help you to get more acquainted with your theme in a visual manner – not to mention it can be a lot of fun to watch movies!

Once your list is finished, you need to split it into categories. Divide your list into four columns with the following headings: People/Characters, Places/Locations, Objects, Actions. Why didn't I have you divide the words into columns as you created the list? I've found if you have to make decisions about what your ideas are (i.e. what category they fall in), although it may only take a second or two of brain energy, it inhibits the brain from free flowing its ideas.

STOP!!!!

Do not continue with the designing process until you have completed the above themed word list assignment. It is crucial that you have your list in front of you as you continue. Feel free to read ahead, if you are curious…but DO NOT attempt to take action in designing your quest until the list is completed. You'll need a comprehensive understanding of the theme you chose. The actual creating of the list provides this nicely. Secondly, you will need a constant source of ideas as you create and your list will become your saving grace at times of creative block. Do not short change yourself by settling for a skimpy list!

At this time, it is important to establish in your own mind the mood you would like to set for your quest. You see, not all quests have the same mood. In some, like a 1930's archeological expedition, you would want to imbue a feeling of adventure and mysticism. In others, like a hunt for vampires, you would want to create a mood closer to fear or terror. The more you've identified the mood in your mind, the better you will be able to create that mood for your guests.

MOVING ON

Now that you have taken the time to develop a terrific list of images, ideas, and objects that relate to your theme, it is time to build the list of possible actions for your 'movie.' Remember the list I did in Chapter 2 about vampires? Keeping your theme in mind, what would be some actions (however impossible they may seem for you to pull off) that would make your movie exciting? Swinging from a rope across a suspension bridge? Sneaking into a high security prison? Weathering a storm on a ship? Write down 10 of the top actions/experiences that would need to be present in your movie to keep your theme alive and exciting. Write these 10 in space number 6 on the worksheet.

It is time to talk a bit about structure. This is perhaps the most difficult part of planning any quest. When watching a movie, you will notice there is usually a character (or team of characters) that has a goal he/she must accomplish. If the task were simple, easy, and without complications, it would make for a very boring movie. Instead, typically the main character(s) meets obstacle after obstacle, constantly changing her plans in order to finally reach her goal. Your adventure should attempt to achieve the same process. Let your adventurers have a single goal, but break it down into two/three smaller goals wherein they can attack each individually. Let me give some examples.

In *Nosferatu*, remember, I had the overall mission of ridding a town of a head vampire and all his minions. In order for the teams to be successful, I told them they must:

- Figure out how to keep from falling under Luther's hypnotic spell when they encounter him,
- Learn how to steal his power, and
- Learn how to escape from his castle once they have done A and B.

As the teams completed each of the three tasks, they knew they were getting closer to finishing. They were encouraged each time they reached a new milestone.

In *Dark Fortune*, I had only two tasks. The storyline revolved around discovering the whereabouts of some lost pirate treasure. Every team was given a map and told that the treasure was found somewhere on it. Teams needed to find out:

1   The longitude of the treasure location and
2   The latitude.

Now don't get me wrong, they needed to overcome a lot to find each of the two parallels, but it was these two tasks that, when completed, would give them success in their mission.

In *In Search of the Holy Grail*, there were two tasks the teams had to accomplish before confronting Morgana (who they knew was in possession of the grail.) The two tasks were:

- Find out where Morgana's lair was and
- Find out how to protect themselves from her evil powers once they confronted her.

Again, each of these tasks took a great amount of time and energy to achieve, but when they had done both, they were ready for the climax, the testing of their skills (discussed more later).

Now take *your* mission/storyline and come up with two or three (preferably three) things *your guests* would have to do in order to achieve their goal. Are they trying to free a prisoner from a French Revolutionary prison? Perhaps their three tasks would be

- Find out which cell the prisoner is in
- Figure out a way to have themselves arrested and thrown in the same prison and
- Learn of a way to escape from the prison.

Notice in the examples I chose, the teams could complete the tasks in any order they wanted and they would still be successful. This is a very important point. This gives the teams the freedom to explore and discover. They will not feel as though they are being manipulated like a puppet on a string, but rather that their decisions and theirs alone will dictate the level of success they will achieve. Additionally, you will find that if your teams are spread around in their actions, your level of congestion at any given stop will decrease. If a team sees a build up of other teams waiting to talk to a character, they are free to move on to another task until things clear up. Isn't this what we do in real life? We have a list of things to do, but as we complete them, we rearrange the order as we go to maximize our efficiency.

Now take your three tasks (two if necessary) and write them in Item 8 of your worksheet.

STOP AGAIN!!!

As before, please do not continue until you have your tasks decided upon. I promise the future decisions will be much more flexible, but the order of these first few are crucial.

OKAY, OKAY…WE'RE MOVING ON

THE CLIMAX

As the name would suggest, this is the exciting 'final scene' of the quest. If there was an ultimate foe to face, this would be the time to face him/her. At this time, you want to provide the ultimate ending to your 'movie.' Take some time to dream up some exciting endings to your quest. In *Nosferatu,* it was the time for the teams at the end of their adventure to face Luther (the Head Vampire) and attempt to defeat him. If they did everything correctly before their encounter, they would know everything they would need to know. In *Dark Fortune*, a pirate previously thought dead was at the treasure site. The teams had to outsmart him in order to escape with the treasure. In *In Search of the Holy Grail*, the climax was when the teams confronted Morgana in her formidable dungeon and had to combat her evil spells.

Beyond being an exciting conclusion to your 'movie', your climax needs to be a time of testing for the teams. Utilize the information that they gathered during their mission to help them succeed during the climax. If you are especially clever, you could put in a couple pitfalls for those teams that took a 'shortcut' or two along the way and did not learn everything they should have.

TIMELINES

Now that you have your three tasks, we can now begin working on the timeline. As best you can, answer the following questions.

        What time will your guests arrive?________

        What time will your actual quest begin? ________

        If planning a preshow, what time will this happen? ________

What time will you gather everyone together to explain the rules? _______

What time will teams begin entering the quest? _______

What time will you want the first place team to return? _______

What time do you want the last place team to return by? _______

What time will you announce the winning team? _______

Once you have answered each of these questions, you will know exactly how much time you have for each segment. For example, if you have 7:20 p.m. slated for when the teams will begin entering the quest, and 8:15 p.m. slated when the first place time will finish, then you know that you have 55 minutes to work  with to enable the teams to achieve their two or three tasks PLUS get through the climax.

Once you have calculated how long your actual quest will be, it is time to break that time down into your tasks and climax. In general, I follow a 15/15/15/10 rule. What this means is if I have three tasks, I have each take 15 minutes to complete and then allow an additional 10 minutes for the finale, the climax. However, there have been times when I have intentionally broken this rule for the sake of variety. Sometimes, I think of an idea for a task that would take quite a bit of time, but I feel so strongly about the idea that it is worth sacrificing time from the other tasks. Once you know how long you want each task to take to complete, put this number next to each task on the worksheet.

TASK DESIGNING

(Repeat this section as needed for each task you have detailed on your worksheet.)

As you begin deciding the details of each task, keep in mind how many minutes you have allotted for a team to get the particular task done. This amount of time needs to include travel time (whether walking or driving), thinking time, discussion time within a group, interaction with a potential character and the time to complete any other action you're demanding from your guests for that particular task.

The first detail to spend time thinking about is how your guests will achieve this certain task. If your task is to obtain a map of town, then you are faced with the question of HOW they will obtain it. Will they buy one? If so, will you provide them with 'currency of the realm' before they get started? Or will they have to earn it in town? If they earn it in town, from whom will they work for to raise the money? Perhaps they will not have any way of 'buying' the map, but rather they must make a deal with the mapmaker. Perhaps they can perform a favor or trade the map for an object they already possess or can easily obtain. Perhaps the map is lost and they must search for it. Whatever details you lay out for your task, keep in mind the amount of time you allotted for your task.

I have developed a tool that has helped me organize and detail a given task in relation to the amount of time it takes to complete it. It involves drawing a schematic of the actions a team must take. Below, I have detailed the actions I decided would be necessary to learn how to combat Luther's hypnotic powers in *Nosferatu*.

> Teams must enter the local tavern where they meet Bella, the tavern keeper. She will not let then hang out in her tavern without buying a drink, so the teams have a seat and place an order for a round with some fake money they were provided with before they started their quest. Upon talking to Bella, they learn that she knows the secret to Luther's hypnotic spell, but will not reveal it unless the team does her a favor in return. She explains that she and her brother Jacob, the town priest, had a terrible falling out 20 years prior and have not spoken to each other since. She has felt bad about the whole thing in recent years and has wanted to apologize, but has been afraid to travel in town as of late, due to the vampires. She agrees to tell the teams all that she knows if they will make the brave trek across town to the church and try to make amends for her with her brother. Once they travel to the church and offer peace with Jacob the priest on behalf of Bella, he gives them a message to take back to his sister. When she reads the

message, she knows that the team did what they were supposed to do and tells them that Luther will offer a hypnotic drink to them. To block the spell, they must drop a piece of wax from a church candle into the chalice before taking a drink.

Whew! That sounds like a lot. However, it rarely took more than 10 or 15 minutes to complete. The same actions can be represented in the following schematic.

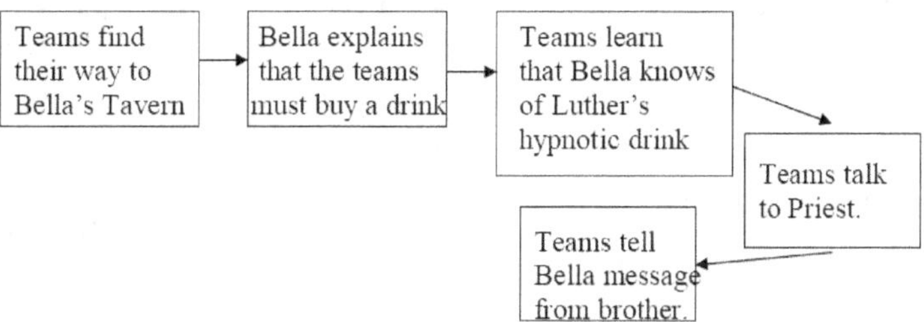

Once you have the schematic, it is easier to organize how much time it will take to complete your task. In the above example, the entire town was confined to the inside of a large warehouse. On the lines connecting the boxes, I wrote the amount of travel time. Now that you know your travel time, within the action boxes write the number of minutes on average it will take to complete each respective action as follows:

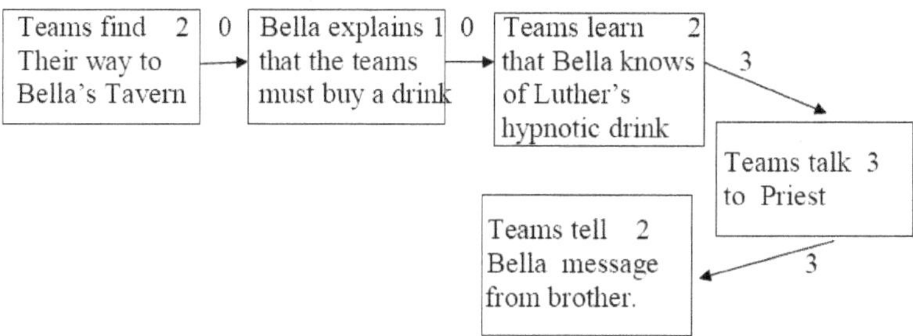

Time yourself doing each action and traveling to and from each location. You might find it takes longer to explain something than you originally thought. Also, keep in mind any waiting time your teams may experience as they wait their turn to speak to a given character. Remember, the more teams there are for a fixed number of characters the longer the waiting times.

Once all your numbers are in place, add them up. Mine, in the above example, added up to 16 minutes. I allowed myself 15 minutes initially, so I was very close and ready to move on to organizing my next task.

Task Design Ideas

There are several different ways for teams to complete a task. Although it depends entirely on the nature of your task, storyline and theme, tasks usually fall into one of two categories: obtain an object or obtain a piece of information.

There is no rule against offering the teams either without any challenges. However, if all your tasks are a matter of going to Point A and picking up an item, then going to Point B and doing the same, your 'movie' will be out right dull for your guests. There are several ways to offer your teams the option of earning the task. In the prior example, teams needed to reconcile a bitter brother/sister relationship before they got what they needed. Other exciting or memorable actions within a task might include:

- Talking to a high profile person (i.e. a government leader, celebrity, high religious official)
- Talking to a wide variety of colorful people (undercover agents or even a drunk)
- Doing favors for a character

- Obtaining items on a list
- Stealing an item from a character (making sure that the character has plenty of items for all teams to steal one)
- Lying to a character, pretending to be someone else.
- Having books set up where they can do a little research (check out several books at a library so that multiple teams can be doing research at once)
- Reuniting a relationship between two characters (playing a go between for communication between the two characters)
- Earning money
- Spending money on an object
- Bribing an official for a special favor
- Delivering a message to a character

These are just a few ways to add a little excitement to the given task.

Organizing Your Climax

Once you have organized and timed your tasks, do the same for your climax. In *Nosferatu*, remember the three tasks were:

1. Figure out how to keep from falling under Luther's hypnotic spell when you encounter him
2. Learn how to steal Luther's power
3. Find out a way to escape from Luther's castle once they've stolen his power

The schematic for the climax looked like this in the following schematic.

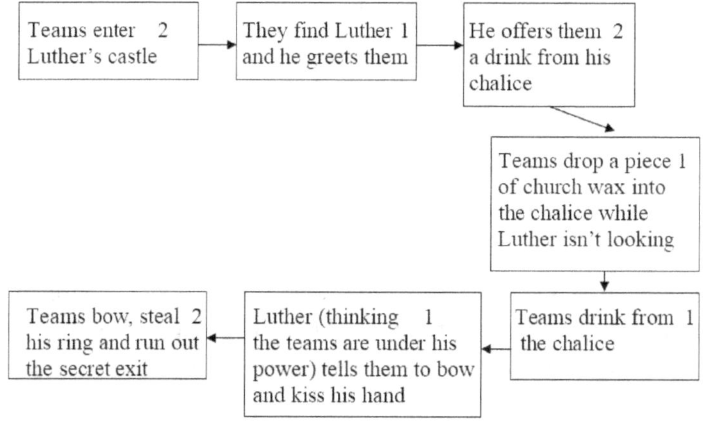

As you can see, if a team failed to complete all three tasks, they would have failed the climax.

In the space provided on the Quest Worksheet, describe your climax and what the teams will encounter once there. Do not forget to include the timing and to keep in mind the amount of time you have originally allotted.

Items List

At this point, the actual designing portion of your quest should be completed. Now it is time to take each task and make, what I call, a detailed Item List. This list will show anything and everything you will need to make it possible for a team to complete the task. In the prior example from *Nosferatu*, my list looked like this:

Tavern Location
- Table and chairs
- Candles on tables
- Cups
- Water for drinks
- Sign for tavern
- Actress playing Bella
- Bella's costume
- Fake money for teams to buy drinks

Church Location
- Sign for church
- Actor to play priest
- Priest costume
- Lots of candles in church (not dripless!)
- Any decorations I can round up to decorate the church

Others
- Map of town for teams to find their way around

Once your list is completed, you will know exactly what you need to put together on the most detailed level. Complete this list for your climax and every task and you have completed your quest design!

At this time, you need to decide on whether or not you are going to have a dramatic introduction and conclusion to your quest, as described in Part II. Include these details on your Items List as well.

Closing

My deepest desire is that after reading this book you're inspired to get creative and set up a quest of your own. It's such an open medium with so many opportunities to create something exciting and unique! A quest even in its simplest form is refreshingly fun. We live in a world that's dominated by screens. Visual effects have never been more realistic. But at the end of the day it's still only a screen. Life is still better lived off the screen and quests are a great way to experience adventure in person.

Create. Live. And have fun, my friend!

Joe Dean

Appendix A - Quest Worksheet

- Who will be coming? ___________________________

  Where will the event take place?

  ____

  ____

  ____

- What type of event will you hold?

  ____

  ____

- How long will the event last? How long will the quest last?

  ____

  ____

- Theme:____
- Storyline/Mission:_____________________________

  ____

  ____

- Actions in your movie:

  ____

  ____

  ____

  ____

  ____

  ____

8. Tasks to overcome the mission

    A.____

    ____

    B.____

    ____

    C.____

    ____

Appendix B - Themes

Government

Mission Impossible/CIA
- A myriad of possible missions are possible… Perhaps they must switch secret microfilm in a top security building.
- They need to flee the country. They must arrange to have passports and other government papers before they are caught by the KGB, et al..
- They must steal something from a high profile government official
- A foreign government is experimenting with human cloning (would work great if you had a set of twins available for volunteering).

FBI
- Teams have to organize a drug bust in an inner city.
- Track down a serial killer.

X-Files
- Someone swears that they were abducted by a UFO. Teams must investigate the case.
- Solve the case if aliens have already landed and have disguised themselves as people.

NASA
- An astronaut for a secret mission has mysteriously disappeared. Teams must form to find where the astronaut is and bring him/her back to NASA.
- Foreign powers are planning to sabotage the newest shuttle mission. The teams are responsible for uncovering the plot and stopping their efforts.

Historical

Ancient Greek/Roman
- Characters and stories from Greek Mythology.

- Teams must stop the assassination of Julius Caesar

Wild Wild West

- Teams have to make a treaty with Indians.
- Teams must deliver official papers to a military outpost explaining that there is a traitor in the ranks.
- Teams must clear a man's name before he is hanged.
- Teams form a posse to find a wanted man.

French Revolution

- Teams must deliver a secret message to England requesting help for the French Aristocrats.
- Teams must find out how to contact the Scarlet Pimpernel to ask his help on a mission.
- Teams must find each of the Three Musketeers to help uncover a plot to assassinate the King.
- Teams sneak into the gallows and free a certain French Aristocrat.

Medieval

- The search for the Holy Grail (the Arthurian legends).
- There is a plot to assassinate the Archbishop. Teams must uncover who it is and why and then tell the King.
- Teams must find Robin Hood's hide out in Sherwood Forrest to elicit his help to uncover a plot to kill the King.

Archeology (Egyptian, Mayan, Aztec, African, Greek/ Roman, Incan)

- Teams must locate the whereabouts of a lost idol.
- They must smuggle an art piece out of the country.
- Recover an artifact from dirty art dealers.

Biblical Times

- Collect certain archeological pieces.

- ■ The Bible is filled with stories and characters for teams to help.

Casablanca

- ■ Teams must try to arrange to either help someone else or themselves get out of Europe in the pre-war and early WWII years.

World War II

- ■ (See Government section for ideas in Nazi Germany).

American Revolution

- ■ Uncover the identity of an English sympathizer within the rebel army
- ■ Warn General Washington of an ambush planned by the British.

Prohibition/Mobsters

- ■ Teams must aid Elliott Ness in an effort to thwart Capone's efforts.
- ■ Perhaps the teams are part of a Mob's family and must find out who the 'rat' is in the 'family.'

American Civil War

- ■ Teams must cross the Mason-Dixon line.
- ■ Teams must find a missing soldier across enemy lines from an affluent family.
- ■ Teams must find the 'Underground Railroad' to warn them that Confederate soldiers are on their way.
- ■ Teams must help a slave(s) through the 'Underground Railroad.'

Settling of the Pilgrims

- ■ Teams must arrange for the American Indians and the European pilgrims to come to peace with one another.

- Perhaps teams start in Europe, and then arrange to find a ship that is sailing for the Americas. They then must land a job in the New World.

Pirates

- Transform the ghost idea from the Halloween section to a quest involving finding the ghosts from a pirate ship that sank. The teams could uncover the story of what happened the night it sank and where to find the treasure that was hidden the day before!
- Teams meet seedy characters in a typical pirate town searching for legendary lost treasure.

California Gold Rush

- Teams find out about rumors of a lost gold mine.
- Teams help a poor gold digger get the deed back for his plot of land before the villain discovers that there is gold there.

Prehistoric

- Teams must converse, or at least try to converse, with early man to find a way back to their own time. (See Time Machine below)

Time Machine

- With this theme, you could use any of the above scenarios.
- Perhaps teams must locate a certain Professor and then enter his time machine to go back in time and then come back after they have achieved a certain task.

Geographical

African Safari

- Perhaps a University Professor is missing in the Belgian Congo and the teams must find him and bring him back to civilization.

- Teams must first find a guide and then search out the entrance to a lost temple.

Ireland

- Teams are entangled in the Northern/Southern Irish conflict.
- Perhaps Leprechauns have been playing horrible tricks on villagers. Teams discover the 'Old World' ways of catching a leprechaun.

Chinese Communism

- Teams must enter Red China to accomplish one of several missions (see Government section)

Drug cartels of Central & South America.

- Work with US and foreign governments to sabotage a smuggling delivery.

Caribbean

- Catch a voodoo witch doctor during Mardi Gras.
- Discover where lost pirate's treasure is located.

Mexico

- Teams must help in the efforts of the Spanish American War.
- Teams side with Zorro to help free Don Diego's father from the Mexican prisons.

South Seas

- An ancient taboo idol must be found for good luck to be restored to the city or event.

Halloween

Frankenstein

- Have to stop Dr. Frankenstein before he finishes bringing his monster to life.
- Have to help Dr. Frankenstein find the monster, keeping on his trail.

Werewolves
- Have to capture him, but you have to make sure that you capture him when he is NOT a wolf!
- Help the Wolfman get a cure to keep him from transforming.

Vampires
- A head vampire has ravaged a small town. They would have to figure out how to defeat him.
- Someone who has been bitten needs a serum to keep from becoming a vampire.

The Mummy
- Someone has freed the Mummy. Teams must find the incantation to trap the Mummy's soul.
- Someone has been captured by the Mummy. Teams must find out where he has taken them and how to defeat him.

Ghosts
- Ghosts from all over time. Teams have to figure out how to send each ghost on to the 'next plane.'
- Teams are looking for a specific ghost (other ghosts help in their quest).

Witches
- Modern day witches have put a spell on the audience/crowd. Teams must find an ancient book to reverse the spell.
- Teams must free an innocent woman from the dangers of the Salem Witch Trials.

On the Trail of Jack the Ripper
- Teams must walk the streets of old London looking for the notorious killer.

Dr. Jeckyl & Mr. Hyde
- Teams must find Dr. Jeckyl before he turns into Mr. Hyde again.
- Teams must help Dr. Jeckyl find a cure for his transformations.

The Legend of Sleepy Hollow
- Teams must find Ichabod Crane to warn him before he makes that fateful trip by horseback.

Zombies

- This one might be a little tricky in that the main allure of a zombie is just to stay alive and to stay ahead of the horde. However, within this theme of staying alive, why not have the teams headed to a secret 'fort' of sorts – a safe haven located somewhere hidden. They have to prove themselves first before they are allowed in, as well.

Miscellaneous

Sinking of the Titanic
- Can meet characters aboard the ship. Perhaps teams have to find a way off the ship before a certain amount of time runs out.
- Transform the ghost idea from the Halloween section to a quest involving finding ghosts from the victims of the horrible tragedy.

Everyone being poisoned
- Begin the evening with a toast. After everyone has had a sip, reveal in a clever way that their drinks have been laced with arsenic. Everyone splits into teams and has to find the antidote within an hour or the poison will have had enough time to reach the heart.

Classical Murder Mystery
- Teams come to the reading of a will, and then someone is murdered. They must figure out who the murderer is.
- Similar to above, but teams are instead coming to a family reunion.

Super Heroes

- Teams meet classic super heroes and help them to defeat the villain of your choice
- As an added touch, give each team member a certain 'power' that will work only once. For instance, one team member can perhaps suspend time when talking to a character (if they have to get past them).

Sherlock Holmes

- Teams must help Watson locate the whereabouts of the missing Holmes.
- Help Holmes solve a case (either a familiar one like The Hound of the Baskervilles, or create one of your own).

Fantasy

- Teams must locate a certain mystical wizard and encounter danger and memorable characters along the way.
- Perhaps two worlds are at war and each team is responsible for bringing peace.

Indiana Jones

- Can easily adapt any of the storylines from the movies or create one of your own.
- Teams must meet one (or all) of the villains from the movies.
- Must retrieve the Cross of Coronado.

Jurassic Park

- Do not be intimidated by this one…although the creation of physical dinosaurs may be a little out of your budget, you can still create a lot of the atmosphere with a great sound system and terrific lighting.
- Teams must find a certain kind of bone sample in the jungle (meet lots of characters that are lost in area and are afraid for their lives).
- (See also Prehistoric in Historical section)

In Search of Bigfoot/Yeti

- Teams must talk with scientists and local eyewitnesses to see if this creature actually exists.
- When the team finds Bigfoot, they must take a picture of it. (Polaroid cameras would work best)

Christmas Carol

- Teams meet all the characters from the Dickens's tale in order to help Scrooge understand Christmas.
- Perhaps Scrooge is framed for Jacob Marley's death. Teams must meet with Scotland Yard and the characters from the story to clear Scrooge's name.

The Lost City of Atlantis

- Teams talk to experts to find the whereabouts of this lost city.
- A professor claims to have found the lost city of Atlantis and brought back some treasure as proof. However, greedy art collectors have captured him. The teams must find him and rescue him.

Kidnapping

- At the event, have one of the guests (one that you have arranged ahead of time) kidnapped right before everyone's eyes. Teams must form to find out who would want to kidnap that particular person and then go after saving them.
- Every team starts out with a ransom note. They must meet forensic specialists to figure out how to save the poor victim.

American Cinema

- A writer who has written a million dollar script has had his original copy stolen. Teams must meet celebrity look-a-likes to find out where the script is located.
- With all the wealth and power of today's movie studios, it should not be hard to come up with a good murder mystery for the teams to play cops with.

- There could be a murder plot to kill a 1920's-30's Hollywood figure. Teams would meet all the black and white, silent movie icons of the past (i.e. Charlie Chaplin, Mabel Normand, etc.)

Computer Technology

- A Hacker has just cracked the IRS database and it is up to the teams to find him before he bankrupts the United States of America.
- A secret microchip is being developed which will enable travelers to be materially transported from one location to another (similar to being 'beamed aboard' in STAR TREK).

Alien Conspiracy

- Teams must figure out who is an alien (posing as a human) in order to uncover a secret plot to take over the Earth.
- Aliens have already come to take over the earth. Guests form in teams with a secret mission ordered by a Human Resistance Coalition against the aliens.

Steampunk

- An inventor has designed the ultimate invention of your choice. Alas, a rival inventor has stolen all of his research and hidden it away to claim ownership of it. Teams will need to figure out not sure where the plans are…but how to steal them back!
- Two inventor guilds are about to go to war. A message of mediation must be delivered to the leader of the opposing guild before fighting begins. However, some inventors want the war to begin (those manufacturing weapons) and will thwart the teams' efforts to bring peace.

Arabian Nights

- Teams must find three genies with special powers to help rid a small kingdom of an evil genie.
- Teams must help the rightful heir as Sultan overthrow the evil Sultan currently in power.

- Aladdin has lost his magic lamp and the teams are in search of it before an enemy finds it first.
- Teams must find the hideout lair of the legendary 40 Thieves of Baghdad and recover something stolen from the Sultan.

Appendix C - Adapting to a Mini-Quest

So, what is a *mini-quest* and why is this section included as an appendix versus being included with the main portion of the book? I'll answer both.

I've termed a mini-quest as a short adventure that typically only includes one task (versus three as we discussed before.) As such, the entire experience typically might last only 15-20 minutes plus any traveling time, if there is any. These are for when you're wanting to plan a short activity that might last only 15-20 minutes from beginning to end. Often times, this is best when you'd like to plan something short and quick for an individual.

Why include the explanation here? Mostly because it was important that I was able to explain what a full quest looks like in its entirety. Now that you understand what that is, understanding that a mini-quest is simply a full-quest with only one task is simple. Because there's only one task, then there's typically no need for a lot of rules, forming teams, pre-shows and post-shows, etc. Even a climax is optional.

In Appendix D I've included a fully fleshed out mini-quest entitled The Hand-Off. It only requires two characters (one character in person and one character that your participant will only interact with on the phone) and a couple locations. It's linear in nature and is best suited for an individual. It's simple and fun and should illustrate what a mini-quest might look like that you can create using the concepts discussed in this book. It's included purely for illustration... However, feel free to photocopy the Appendix D and you'll have everything you'll need to actually set it up!

Appendix D - The Hand-Off

This will step you through the creation of a very simple mini-quest. It's very short and not very complex (as Quests go, that is…). However, once you step through the process and set up this adventure, you'll have a much better understanding of what a Quest is and their potential for REAL life adventure for you and your family and friends. It's a working mini-quest that you can actually set up for someone (or use it as an episode of sorts within a full quest you design yourself.)

Let's begin with the theme. For this mini-quest, I chose an Indiana Jones style, dirty art dealer encounter adventure. For the sake of illustration, let's set it up for our good friend 'Bob.' Bob's a good natured guy who likes to have fun and who's a big Indiana Jones fan, which is a bonus for us (which helped pick our theme.) It's Bob's birthday and I want to give Bob a unique experience for finding his way to his surprise birthday party. All he knows is that I asked him to reserve the night for me and that I have something special planned for him. Although I've designed some quests that take weeks to experience, this particular experience will take approximately an hour for Bob (if you add the traveling time.)

The following is a narrative to explain exactly what will happen to our friend Bob that night. Of course, some variables might be a little different based on some minor choices that Bob makes, however the overall story and experience will remain the same.

The Hand Off

On the Wednesday before the Saturday night party, Bob received a mysterious package in the mail, with postage from Honduras. Inside was a small, decorative gold box and a short note that simply said "I doubt I'll be able to make the delivery…you're probably going to have to take it to the buyer for me. I'll contact you later. Jared." Along with the message was some writing that Bob couldn't make out.

Puzzled by the package, Bob holds onto it and takes it to work with him, showing his co-workers the gold box and the note. Knowing his birthday was only days away, he begins to guess that it has something to with it. He approaches his friends, too, but no one fesses up to knowing anything about it.

Now remember, we arranged in advance to take Bob out for his birthday so he's expecting a casual hang out time that evening…little does he know that a party is waiting for him. That Saturday morning, Bob gets a call on his cell phone. It's Jared. Jared explains that he's still delayed in Central America and can't make the trade. Bob is confused at first as he has no idea who Jared is or why he pulled Bob into his business. Jared then explains that Bob will need to meet the buyer at 4:00 pm at a designated spot about 15 minutes from Bob's home and that in return, the buyer will give him an envelope containing further instructions. Realizing that 4:00 is coincidentally the time that we were scheduled to meet up with him for his birthday, Bob puts the pieces together and realizes that we're behind it all.

Playing along, Bob says that he'll agree to make the delivery to the buyer. Jared thanks Bob, but not before warning him that the buyer, known only as The Doctor, is a bit 'rough' and that Bob should be a little careful when dealing with him. He then explains to Bob that he needs to first go to a drop off point to pick up the translator code for the message that Jared originally sent. It turns out that The Doctor prefers to authenticate all messengers by requiring pass codes for all transactions. Jared gives Bob a phone number to call The Doctor directly to find out where the pass code will be delivered.

A little nervous, Bob hangs up and begins to dial the number for The Doctor. When the other line picks up, a deep voice answers and Bob explains the call he received. The Doctor says that he doesn't like last minute changes and is a little reluctant to continue with the transaction. He finally agrees and details a park in the city and a specific park bench. He explains that he'll have one of his 'men' drop off the pass code there by 3:00 that afternoon.

Bob, a little excited now, begins to plan his day, making sure he gets to the park at a little after 3:00. Once there, he finds the exact park bench described by The Doctor and reaches underneath as instructed. Sure enough, he finds a small envelope which he nonchalantly tucks in his pocket and heads back to his car. Upon opening the envelope, he removes a small piece of paper with writing similar to those he saw on the letter originally sent by Jared. Next to each character is a letter of the alphabet. With this in hand, Bob is able to translate the original note to reveal the phrase "Crockett fell at the Alamo." Not sure if it meant anything, Bob committed it to memory just in case.

At 4:05, Bob arrives at the meeting place described by Jared to hook up with The Doctor, an outdoor café. Bob was a few minutes late because he had some trouble finding parking. After The Doctor warily warns Bob that he's not accustomed to be kept waiting, he asks Bob for the pass code. Bob says "Crockett fell at the Alamo." With this, The Doctor smiles and asks for the box and Bob hands it to him.

The Doctor begins to hand Bob a sealed envelope while relishing the view of his new treasure in his hands. Before he completely hands it over to Bob, though, his face turns to a puzzled frown and puts the envelope pack in his pocket. There's something about the treasure that isn't right. "This is a fake! You honestly tried to pass off a fake?" The Doctor stares down Bob while Bob fumbles to figure out what to say next. "Are you trying to double cross me? Did you think that I wouldn't notice?" The Doctor continues to drill Bob.

Thinking quick, Bob gets the idea to call Jared (Jared's number still in Bob's phone from the call earlier in the day.) Bob explains to Jared the situation and Jared asks to be put on speaker as Jared speaks "Hey Doc! Well, you can't blame a guy for tryin'! Alright, I put the real box in the planter 10 feet from where you're sitting. I arranged for the real one to be placed there earlier this afternoon. Go easy on Bob, he wasn't wise to the switch."

With this, The Doctor walks over to the planter as described by Jared and finds an identical box. He examines it cautiously, then seems relieved at what he holds in his hands. He then walks over to Bob, hands him the envelope he took out earlier and smiles. "I can never trust that scoundrel, but he always delivers…" He hands Bob the first box (the fake) and says "Here, you can keep this, too. Consider it a souvenir for the day…" and walks away on the crowded sidewalk.

Bob opens the envelope and in it are directions to the location where his surprise birthday party is. Upon arriving at the party, everyone is anxious to greet him…and he's anxious to find us to ask how we arranged such a cool experience!

Now…let's explain how to pull it off!

What you'll need:
1. Make a copy of DOCUMENTS 1-4. There you'll find notes for the volunteers playing Jared and The Doctor. Also, you'll find the note that gets mailed along with the pass code that your adventurer will find in the park (or other location of your choice.)
2. Read through the two character sheets so that you fully understand what the two volunteers are expected to do in case they have any questions. Also, in the appropriate spaces on the character sheets, fill in the appropriate blanks that are specific to your city (where your adventurer will find the coder and where the hand off will take place, the times, etc.)
3. Two cheap dollar store jewelry boxes (two identical ones – preferably ones that are decorative and have some weight to them.)
4. Some gold spray paint
5. An envelope with a note to hand to the adventurer from The Doctor at the end of the hand off (this one is optional.)

To Do:
1. Paint the two small boxes with the gold spray paint (a couple coats for extra gloss.)
2. Take one of the boxes and wrap it in a mailing box, along with the note from Jared with the Asian writing
3. Find two different volunteers to play Jared and The Doctor. It's preferable that your two volunteers are NOT known by your adventurer, to make the experience more 'real.' Hand the instruction sheets from DOCUMENTS 1 & 2 to each of your respective volunteers and explain their parts.
4. PRACTICE with your two volunteers in advance so that they feel comfortable. You want them to be natural with it.
5. A week before your adventurer is to experience the Quest, arrange for them to receive the package with the gold box and the note (leaving it on their front porch, having someone strange hand deliver it to their workplace, mailing it via US postal, etc.)

Voila! You're all set. Ready to start the adventure.

On the day of the Quest, make sure your Jared volunteer calls your adventurer as described. Also, make sure that you place the coder paper (inside an envelope optional) at the spot you told Jared to explain on the phone BEFORE the time also detailed.

Arrange for your Doctor volunteer to arrive at the hand off location you've chosen early so that you can answer any last minute questions and so that you can find a safe place to watch the fun. Also, make sure that you hide the second gold box in a safe place near where the hand off will take place. Finally, call your Jared volunteer (who's awaiting your call) to explain exactly where you placed the second gold box so that he can detail the location in his phone conversation toward the end of the mini-quest.

Once your adventurer arrives, you're all set to watch the fun. Once The Doctor leaves, you can either choose to reveal yourself, or stay hidden in case you have something planned (per the note you had The Doctor hand them.)

It's an amazing experience, with little set up. It takes a lot of written 'words' to explain the scenario, but when it's played out, it's really quite simple...to set up. You're adventurer will have a great time, even through the awkwardness of seemingly handing the dirty art dealer a fake!

For added fun, consider the following extra ideas:
    * Have a big guy dressed like a thug stand behind your Doctor character the entire time. They don't need to say a word, only look menacing.
    * Video the experience so that your adventurer can watch it later

There are four separate sheets of paper to copy.

1.   Character sheet for your Jared volunteer – Familiarize yourself with the instructions. Make sure you detail exactly when they are to call your adventurer and when they can expect a call from you on that day detailing the exact location of the second gold box (so that they can await the other phone call from your adventurer soon after.)

2.   Character sheet for your Doctor volunteer – Familiarize yourself with the instructions. You may want to practice with them a little beforehand so that they understand (and remember) their part. Additionally, make sure you detail on the sheet exactly where you'll hide the coder piece of paper (having scouted out a location in advance.)

3.   Note to accompany gold box mailing – For added fun, you might consider rewriting the note in personal handwriting (including the coding.) Although not necessary, it will had a realistic feel to the delivery.

4.   Decoder to be found by your adventurer that day. This can be put in a envelope if desired, but not necessary. If placing it outside, you might consider placing it inside a sandwich baggie so that it stays dry. MAKE SURE THAT YOU DON'T HIDE THE CODER WHERE OTHERS WILL SEE YOU OR THERE IS A CHANCE OF IT BEING TAKEN!!! The Quest hinges on that coder being there when your adventurer arrives to get it (which is why it's suggested to place the coder at the last possible hour before it's found.)

Jared

There are three separate phone conversations that make up your portion of the adventure.

Phone Call #1:   The call to the adventurer.   You will call _______________ (*name of adventurer*) on _______________ (*date*) at exactly _____________ (*time*.) In that phone conversation, you will say the following:

"Hey, this is Jared. Did you get my package? Listen, I desperately need you to help save my skin. I promised to deliver that gold box I stole from a Meso-American temple here in Honduras to a buyer on _____________ (*date of the adventure.*) I ran into trouble here and I still haven't been able to leave the country. If that box isn't delivered to the buyer by that time, I'm a dead man. Will you help me?"

Don't proceed until they agree. Once they do, say

"Perfect. This is what you'll do. I only know the buyer as The Doctor, as it would seem he likes his anonymity. Here's his phone number _______________ (*phone number for volunteer playing The Doctor*). You'll need to call him to ask him where you can find the decoder. You see, he's a little 'cautious' and requires all exchanges to begin with a coded message, for security reasons. Just tell him that you're making the exchange instead of me, he'll explain where he'll have the coder placed. Then, get the coder and translate the message that I sent. That is what he'll need before he'll deal. Understand?"

Make sure they understand and, just before you hang up, say "And… uh…be careful, eh?"

Phone Call #2 – The call from the person setting up the adventure just before the actual hand off is to take place. They will the exact location of the gold box you'll need for Call #3. Write it down so that you can accurately relay the information in the next call.

Phone Call #3 – The frantic call from the adventurer during the hand-off. You see, in the adventure story, you sent them a fake box and tried to have them pass it off to the buyer. They will have gotten caught and will call you to find out what to do. They could be in any number of states when they call (worried, angry, sheepish, etc.) Simply reply with "Put me on so that The Doctor can hear, too." Once you know they both can hear, say:

"Hey Doc! Well, you can't blame a guy for tryin'! Alright, I put the real box (*detail here the location you wrote down from Phone Call #2*). I arranged for the real one to be placed there earlier this afternoon. Go easy on Bob, he wasn't wise to the switch." The person playing The Doctor will walk over to the location you detail and say "You're a scoundrel, Jared, but you always deliver" at which point you reply with "Of course. Hey, _______________ (*name of person on adventure*) no hard feelings, eh?" Then hang up.

The Doctor

There are two separate interactions that make up your portion of the adventure.

The Phone Call – You will receive a phone call early on the day of the adventure. The adventurer will call you explaining that they will be making a hand off to you that you were expecting from Jared. They should also explain that they need to know where they can find the coder for the exchange. When they call and explain the situation, say:

"I don't like last minute changes…but I'm really looking forward to getting my hand on the piece. I'll have one of my associates drop off the coder sometime before ______________ (*earliest time that adventurer can pick up coder*) at ________________ (*exact spot where the coder will be placed.*) Once you have it, meet me at ______________ __________________ (*exact location where the hand off will take place.*) Understand?"

Once they affirm they got the information, hang up.

The Actual Hand Off – You will be waiting at the location you explained in your phone conversation to them EARLY so that you are there before they arrive. Once there, understand where the person setting up the adventure hides the second gold box so that you can retrieve it later during the interaction. In your pocket will probably be an envelope with a note (if the person setting up the adventure has something for you to give the adventurer at the end of the exchange.)

When the adventurer approaches, they will say "Crockett fell at the Alamo" at which time you will look serious and ask "Do you have the item?" Do not speak to them UNTIL they say the Crockett line. When they give it to you, look happy at first, but then carefully examine the gold box they give you and turn your smile to a face of concern. Then look up at the adventurer and say

"It's a fake! Did you really think that you could fool me!" Wait for them to squirm a little. Then say in an angry tone "I'm going get Jared for this…the question is, what do I do about you?"

If they don't already suggest it themselves, tell them that it would be a good idea for them to call Jared for some answers. They will have a short conversation with Jared, while you continue to look angry. The adventurer will then hold up the phone so that you can hear Jared explain where he hid the 'real' gold box. Go over to the location (it will be the place that the person setting up the location hid it earlier) and pull it out. Examine it carefully then smile calling out to Jared (still on the phone)

"You're a scoundrel, Jared, but you always deliver."

Continue smiling at the box until the adventurer ends their conversation with Jared. At this time hand the adventurer the envelope (if the person setting up the adventure has one for you to give) and then give them the 'fake' box they handed you earlier and say "Here, you can keep this…I'm afraid it's not worth more than a cheap souvenir."

And with that, walk away and leave, not looking back...

时谊行时先天由由
帖天天小
生由
由西天
生小生协行.

A	生
B	圣
C	时
D	市
E	天
F	帖
G	文
H	西
I	喜
J	夏
K	先
L	小
M	协
N	新
O	行
P	学
Q	宴
R	谊
S	迎
T	由
U	友
V	于
W	愉
X	圆
Y	月
Z	在